Reading for Meaning: Selected Teaching Strategies

Valerie Meyer, Ph.D.

Southern Illinois University at Edwardsville

Donald Keefe, Ph.D.

Southern Illinois University at Edwardsville

LIFELONG LEARNING BOOKS
Teacher Resource Series
Scott, Foresman and Company
Glenview, Illinois • London

Library of Congress Cataloging-in-Publication Data
Meyer, Valerie.
    Reading for meaning : selected teaching strategies / Valerie
Meyer, Donald Keefe.
        p.   cm. -- (Teacher resource series)
    "Lifelong learning books."
    Bibliography: p.
    Includes index.
    ISBN 0-673-24242-0
    1. Reading--United States--Remedial teaching. 2. Reading (Adult educa-
tion)--United States. 3. Reading--United States--Ability testing. I. Keefe,
Donald. II. Title. III. Series.
LB1050.5.M48   1990
428.4'2--dc20   89-10238
                                                                            CIP

ISBN 0-673-24242-0

Printed in the United States of America
    3 4 5 6 MAL 94 93 92

*We wish to dedicate this book
with love to Marcellite Sellinger.*

ABOUT THIS BOOK

This book is a "recipe" book of reading strategies for adult literacy coordinators, adult literacy tutors, ABE (adult basic education)/GED instructors, junior high school and high school reading teachers, teachers of English as a second language, and anyone else who works with adolescents and adults who are experiencing difficulty reading. The book begins with a brief explanation of the psycholinguistic theory of reading, upon which the forty reading strategies described here are based.

The authors have outlined four profiles of learners experiencing reading difficulties. These profiles range from nonreaders (Profile One) to readers who need some fine tuning in preparation for the GED Test (Profile Four). You should be able to identify your reader with one of these four profiles by comparing your reader's weaknesses and strengths with those given in the profile descriptions. The learning strategies most appropriate for your reader can be found on the pages following the profile you choose.

All reading strategies described in this book have been tried and tested by volunteer tutors, ABE teachers, and graduate students serving as reading clinic tutors under the authors' supervision. The learners who were taught with these strategies improved an average of three years (as measured by standardized reading achievement tests) after three to six months of ninety-minute tutoring sessions per week.

CONTENTS

PREFACE

*I've been a literacy volunteer for about six months. The
learner I tutor doesn't seem to be making much progress.
I know he's really trying—I'm really trying too. Do you
have any suggestions? Here's what we've been doing. . . .*

Questions and conversations like this are common ones for us. For
the past several years we have been involved with adult basic education
(ABE) instructors, volunteer tutors, and others concerned about the best
way to teach adults and adolescents to read. This book evolved from
their concerns and our attempts to provide assistance.

Several years ago we organized our community's first literacy volunteer effort. We provided twenty-one hours of training to fourteen willing
and capable volunteers. The volunteers were matched with learners
who had a myriad of reading disabilities. As we watched the progress
of the tutors and their students, we began to see a void in our tutoring
scheme. Many of the learners being tutored had problems that required
diagnosis beyond the expertise of a volunteer tutor. One man needed
glasses, but his problem was not identified until he had been tutored
almost four months. A second needed a hearing aid. A third was tutored
for almost a year but made almost no progress.

It was apparent that the students of our volunteers needed a thorough
professional diagnosis of their reading problems. Practical teaching
techniques, often the core of most volunteer training and teachers'
workshops, were fine—but our volunteers needed more. We realized
that they also needed adequate diagnostic testing.

In 1986 we received funding from the Office of the Illinois Secretary
of State to establish a diagnostic center for adults. This book stems from
research we have conducted with over two hundred individuals with
reading disabilities. The population we served ranged in age from
sixteen to seventy-six years. We conducted in-depth, individualized
diagnostic assessments and provided instructional suggestions based
upon our assessment results. Our diagnosticians included a team of
current and former graduate students majoring in reading. In addition
to expertise in reading, many of these diagnosticians had undergraduate
teaching majors in fields such as speech and hearing, special education,
and educational psychology.

The diagnostic tests used with each client varied, but generally they
included the Keystone School Vision Screening Test (1972), the Wepman

Auditory Discrimination Test (1986), the Basic Reading Inventory (Johns 1985), the Burke Reading Interview, the Slosson Intelligence Test (1984; this was used to determine general strengths and weaknesses in academic areas, not as a measurement of IQ), and an informal silent reading inventory designed by us. Screening tests based upon Jordan's *Dyslexia in the Classroom* (1977) were administered when it was felt such instruments were appropriate.

We have often been asked if we were really comfortable with our selection of test instruments. The answer is yes and no. We feel that, given the variety of tests used plus additional information from tutors, we were able to make adequate assessments. However, most of the test instruments used were not designed for adults; therefore, we sometimes questioned their validity and relied more upon our professional judgement.

Test scores should *always* be used cautiously. Many things affect test performance: factors such as possible vision problems, hearing problems, fatigue, medication, lighting, and even the comfort of a reader play important roles in assessing the reader's ability. Whereas test scores *may* reflect a reading disability, it's important to consider the *cause* of the problems. More important than specific tests, we feel the key to sound diagnosis in our research—and in general—was and is the observational expertise of the person conducting the testing.

As we reviewed our reports and suggested teaching strategies, distinct patterns emerged. The learners ranged in abilities from those who could not read at all to those who needed just a bit of help to pass the GED Test. Four profile categories became evident. These profiles are explained in detail in this book, along with abstracts of sample diagnostic reports and teaching strategies.

The four profiles are *not* meant to be cast in stone. Our experience is that volunteer tutors, ABE instructors, special education, junior high, and high school teachers will identify with our profiles and find their students among them. Our attempt is not to typecast these learners; we sought only to create characteristic profiles that would make sense to those involved in literacy instruction.

Without the assistance of our graduate students, this research would never have been possible. We wish to thank Joyce Anders, Marilyn Bodnam, Randi Brown-Hattery, Karen Cooper, Marsha Cremer, Margaret Drew, Julie Harvey, Marty Eisloeffel, Claudette Graetz, LaDarla Hawks, Margene Jerrolds, Gail Miller, Beth Rull, Barbara Saul, Teena Townzen, and Jacqueline Tolbert. We would also like to thank Mary Ann Nickel, for her helpful comments as we were writing our manuscript, and Mary Jo Peck and Colleen Fields, for their assistance with typing and editing.

A NOTE ON TERMINOLOGY

The diagnostic profiles and teaching strategies presented in this book are intended to serve classroom teachers at the junior high and high school level, adult basic education (ABE) instructors, and volunteer tutors. We do not presume our audience has necessarily had formal training in how to teach reading. Therefore, certain terms used in this book are defined below so that our intent is not misunderstood.

Grade level:
This term is used to provide a common reference point to discuss reading problems. Grade levels must be used cautiously. They are never unchangeable numbers because comprehension depends upon the reader's life experiences and knowledge of language. A passage that is easily comprehended by one capable reader may be totally misunderstood by another capable reader who lacks some prior knowledge of the topic.

Independent level:
This term is also used as a common reference point; it refers to what one can read with no assistance. This level, too, varies with what a reader already knows about a particular subject.

Instructional level:
This term refers to the level at which a learner can read with the assistance of an instructor. We use this term in an effort to provide guidance in selecting materials for readers. A reader's knowledge about a topic and his or her interest in the topic will best determine the choice of instructional materials.

Listening-capacity level:
We use this term cautiously for lack of a better one. Poor readers generally score poorly on traditional measures of intelligence and capacity. We equate listening with capacity in an effort to provide guidance in setting realistic expectations for those working with learners who have reading problems. Listening levels are determined by reading aloud to the person being tested. The grade level at which a learner can listen and retell with about 70 percent accuracy was determined to be the listening-capacity level. Like independent and instruc-

tional levels, the listening-capacity level is not fixed. It improves as a learner becomes more adept in using language.

Instructor/learner:

We use these terms throughout the book. The word *instructor* may refer to a volunteer literacy tutor, a school teacher, an ABE instructor, or anyone else in the role of assisting someone learning to read. The word *learner* refers to the person who receives reading instruction.

1

The Adult Learner

ADULTS AND OLDER ADOLESCENTS differ greatly from children. For one thing, these learners have a great deal of competition for their time. **They have responsibilities far exceeding those of young children. These responsibilities often compete with their desire to learn.** An adult learner may miss a class or a tutoring session not out of lack of desire or neglect but because of family and work responsibilities. Good reading instructors are quick to acquaint themselves with their learners' interests, problems, and lifestyles.

> Warren was frequently thirty or forty minutes late for his tutoring session. His tutor would pace the floor and complain that Warren was irresponsible and inconsiderate. When Warren would finally arrive, his tutor's patience was worn thin. A brief discussion about this situation revealed that Warren's car was very old and often broke down. The situation was resolved simply by scheduling sessions in a library close to Warren's home, which he could walk to if necessary.

Many learners with reading problems may also have an undiagnosed vision or hearing problem. Unlike young children, these learners may not have had a vision or hearing test for years. The glasses they wear may be an outdated prescription or belong to a friend. It is extremely important, whenever possible, to provide for hearing and vision exams.

> Juanita had been attending an ABE class for over six months. Her attendance was good and motivation excellent. Often, though, she complained of headaches, which she attributed to sinus problems. Her instructor suspected something else. A local school nurse, asked to conduct a vision screening with Juanita, found vision problems. One week

later with the assistance of a local organization, Juanita had glasses, her headaches were gone, and she was free to concentrate on learning.

While obtaining a hearing aid or glasses will not automatically solve a reading problem, one barrier will have been removed. (Some community organizations help provide glasses and hearing aids for individuals who cannot afford to pay for such services. These organizations vary in each community; contact a local physician's office for more information.)

Older adolescents and adults are impatient learners. Most seek reading instruction for very specific reasons—and they do not want to spend the rest of their lives learning to read. Commercial materials are extremely useful, but they should be used in conjunction with real-world materials that match the specific needs of individual learners. Many adults have experienced a crisis in their lives that caused them to seek assistance. Therefore, it's important to know a learner's immediate reading needs.

> When Robert called a local volunteer program, his voice was insecure and tense. He explained he had just refused to put his name in for promotion. This was the third time he passed up the possibility of promotion because he was unable to read the work orders at his plant. Tired of hiding his illiteracy, Robert decided to seek help.

Many learners who have reading problems also have a history of repeated failures in educational settings. They need and want instructors who treat them as adults in a supportive environment.

> Sheryl missed most of first and second grade because of illness in her family. When she finally returned to school, she was forced to attend first grade. A tall child, she was often uncomfortable in a desk which was too small. In addition, classmates frequently ridiculed her on the playground. As an adult, deciding to return to school was not an easy decision for Sheryl to make because she was afraid of being ridiculed again.

Most adults and older adolescents with reading disabilities have a well-developed sense of oral language. They have compensated for a lack of reading skills by focusing on their listening and speaking skills. Because of this and their life experiences, they possess a rich bank of concepts and real-life knowledge that makes them easier to teach than children. It is important to use these oral and experiential strengths to remediate the weakness of dealing with print.

> Tom had worked for a landscaper for over a decade. His green thumb and sense of artistry made him popular with local retailers who used flowers and plants in their displays. His tutor used the language-

experience approach to help Tom compose and read a short manual about how to care for plants. His customers were delighted to receive this information, never suspecting the manual was part of Tom's reading lesson.

These learners, unlike young children, are generally able to explain what seems to work best and why—they can observe and relate their own progress. It is important to listen carefully and respond to their comments, since they often will diagnose their own problems. This self-diagnosis is invaluable.

> Samella was enrolled in several high school remedial classes. Social studies was giving her an especially hard time. She approached her instructor and said, "I do just fine when I have to read a paragraph and answer the question. It's these other questions, the ones with the circles and lines, that get me messed up." Her instructor realized Samella needed more direct instruction in reading charts and graphs. Once this was explained to her, Samella's work in social studies improved rapidly.

Of all the things to keep in mind as an instructor, the most important is that adults and older adolescents learn best when the learning environment meets their needs and the atmosphere is one of mutual respect and concern.

Older learners—

- Have other responsibilities that young children do not have
- Are impatient learners
- May have vision or auditory discrimination problems
- Often have histories of repeated failures in educational settings
- Usually have well-developed oral language skills
- Are able to explain what seems to work best and why

CONVERSATION SUGGESTIONS

What about the critical first encounter with an adult or older adolescent who seeks assistance with reading? Where does one begin? What should be talked about? What is important for an adult learner to know as instruction begins? The following suggestions are helpful to keep in mind, especially for new instructors.

Let the learner know he or she is not alone. Many students are unaware that millions of others like themselves have reading problems. Many learners are reluctant to seek help because they fear they are the only ones who cannot read in a society where "everyone" knows how to read. When learners understand that millions of others share their problem, they often feel a great deal of relief.

Discuss the fact that learning to read does not happen all at once. When we learn a new skill, there are days when we're not as proficient as the day before. The analogy of a child learning to walk may be helpful. It does not happen all at once; the child takes a few steps, then falls, takes a few more, then falls. These small steps are all part of the process. Most learners will have these lapses. They are to be expected. Talking about them *before* they occur will ease the frustration *when* they occur.

Learning to read requires a commitment of time and endurance. A frank discussion about the amount of effort required is essential. A learner needs to commit to a minimum of seven hours per week during which he or she will be engaged in meaningful encounters with print. This does not mean a learner must be *tutored* seven hours per week but rather must *practice* a minimum of seven hours.

Individuals who are unable to read much by themselves might be expected to listen to a tape of a story and follow along, to circle words they know in a newspaper, or to copy the names of foods in their refrigerator. More advanced readers should practice reading independently a minimum of one hour a day. Their practice materials need not be textbooks; newspapers, magazines, and paperbacks provide ample reading matter. The only way to become a proficient reader is to read.

Encourage the learner to be open and honest about his or her progress. Many students are timid and extremely reluctant to voice their opinions about the materials or programs they are assigned. Often, rather than say they do not like a particular book or reading series, they continue until they get bored and lose motivation, or they simply drop out of the program. Therefore, discussing these issues *first* helps if a problem arises.

Let the learner know you have experience in teaching reading or that you have received special training to do so. The idea is to develop a relationship of confidence and trust.

These conversation suggestions are not meant to be inclusive. You may want to add your own ideas to this list.

Finally, a note of caution: Not all reading instructors and their learners are a perfect match. If you are a volunteer tutor who feels uncomfortable with the person you've been assigned to teach, or if you feel you cannot help that person, contact your coordinator or supervisor and explain the situation. Request to be assigned to another learner. If you are an ABE instructor, talk the situation over with a colleague; perhaps there are options you have not thought about. Learning will not take place in an environment that is not friendly and optimistic.

C H A P T E R

2

The Theory
Behind the Strategies

THIS HANDBOOK IS meant to be a practical "recipe" book for ABE/GED instructors, adult literacy volunteer tutors, special-education teachers, and high school teachers who work with older adolescents and adults. To fully understand and successfully implement the strategies in this book, it is important to understand the theory upon which the strategies are based. In other words, it is necessary to know *why* a strategy will work as well as *what* the strategy is.

The psycholinguistic theory developed and popularized by Ken and Yetta Goodman (1987), Carolyn Burke (1985), Constance Weaver (1988), and Frank Smith (1985) underlies the explanation of the reading process and strategies presented in this book. (If you'd like to learn more about comprehension and reading theory, you'll find specific books recommended under Suggested Readings.)

WHAT IS READING?

Psycholinguists have described reading as a process that is "only incidentally visual" (Smith 1985). Comprehension depends greatly upon how much a reader already knows about a topic. For instance, if you are a veteran bass fisherman, you will easily understand an article about surface lures; but if you are a novice, you will have to read more carefully.

What happens when a reader's experience and knowledge do not match those of a writer? Comprehension is lost.

> A young man was teaching himself how to bake sugar cookies. The cookies were a failure. He said, "I really couldn't figure out this recipe. It said to separate the eggs. I left one on the counter and put the other on the table. What was I supposed to do after they were separated?"

This gap between the knowledge of the reader and the knowledge of the writer caused a problem in comprehension.

A match between reader and writer is the first prerequisite for comprehension. Therefore, a learner must help choose the materials he or she will be reading.

HOW COMPREHENSION HAPPENS

Comprehension is a process in which readers **sample, predict, confirm,** and ultimately **integrate** text. Good readers do all this almost unconsciously. Poor readers must be taught this four-step process.

Sampling is what you do when you open the Sunday newspaper. You quickly glance at the headlines and leaf through the various parts of the paper. You scan the ads, sports, travel, and other sections to determine which you will read first. Sampling is also what you do when you first look at a book to decide if you want to buy it. You read the reviews and the synopsis of the story on the jacket, and you sample the first few pages to see if you like the style, tone, and subject of the text. You also sample content-area texts by thumbing through the pages to look at the pictures, graphs, charts, and headings so that you have a notion about the topic before reading the pages.

Sampling, then, is what you do *before* you read something to see whether it contains what you are after. It allows you to selectively choose what you read and sets the stage for predicting.

Predicting is the next step in the comprehension process, in which you anticipate what the text will say. When you predict, you guess what will happen in the novel or story you are reading. Predicting is using what you already know to infer what an author will say. You think before you see, so that the alternatives you will have to deal with are dramatically reduced.

As an example, provide the missing letters in this sentence: "He had eggs and b _ _ _ _ for breakfast along with two slices of toast." What word did you supply? Most likely, you guessed *bacon*. How did you do this? Your brain selected the obvious alternative. Your experiences of what people usually eat for breakfast and your use of language made it easy to predict *bacon*.

A more dramatic example of how the brain can predict and make meaning prior to seeing print is provided by the following sentence, which most readers have read or typed sometime in their life. It has sixteen words, each blank indicating a letter:

___   __   ___   ____   ___   ___   ____   ___   __   ____   __

___   ___   __   _____   _____.

Can you predict what the sentence reads? Here is a clue: The first word begins with *N*. Have you guessed the sentence yet? Here is a second clue: The last word begins with *c*. Has that helped? If not, here are two final clues: The first word is *Now* and the last world is *country*. If you have never studied typing, you may still be confused, but most readers would have guessed the sentence "Now is the time for all good men to come to the aid of their country."

If the brain has some prior knowledge, it quickly reduces the amount of print that must be seen to obtain meaning. Predicting is a continual process; it moves the reader along as he or she encounters print. Good readers are always predicting, always asking themselves questions. Poor readers do not know how to do this.

Confirming follows predicting—it is what you do automatically after you have predicted. Essentially, confirming answers your questions. Good readers read to confirm their predictions as naturally as they predict a light will turn off when they flip the switch. If your predictions about a story are correct, you move on to the next part of the text, setting up new predictions. If your predictions are incorrect, you stop and reread to determine what went wrong.

Here is an example of how the process works. Suppose you like to bake (and eat) peanut butter cookies. You notice a recipe for peanut butter cookies in your local newspaper, in which you read the following list of ingredients:

½ cup brown sugar
¼ cup granulated sugar
½ cup soft butter
1 cup peanut butter
½ teaspoon soda
1 tablespoon chili powder
1 ½ cups flour

As you read through the list of ingredients, you probably compared the ingredients and quantities with those you normally use. But something different happens. You read "1 tablespoon chili powder." Because you had not predicted that chili powder would be an ingredient in peanut butter cookies, you glance again at the title. If the title is "Spicy Hot Peanut Butter Cookies," you have found a reason for chili powder's inclusion in the recipe. If the title is "Grandma's Favorite Peanut Butter Cookies," you know that either grandma made a strange cookie or, more likely, there is an error in the recipe.

Good readers confirm spontaneously. But, because poor readers do not make predictions, they fail to read purposefully to confirm. They might not even question the inclusion of chili powder in the recipe!

Integrating completes the process of comprehension. You integrate what you have learned from your reading with what you already know. Piaget used the terms *assimilation* and *accommodation* to describe this process (Ginsburg and Opper, 1969). If you had prior knowledge about what you read, and if the information you gained from reading accurately matched that knowledge, you simply assimilate what you read into what you already know. For example, if you have a three-speed bike and are interested in purchasing a ten-speed, your reading about the ten-speed bike would fit your schema of a three-speed bike fairly closely (each has different gears for different speeds, but a ten-speed bike has more of them).

However, sometimes the category you have in your head about a particular subject does not fit the new information you read. Then you must expand and adapt the existing category to accommodate the new information. If you read, for example, about a bike with no chains or sprockets but with pedals that go up and down on a centrifugal force liquid counter wheel, you have to change your concept of *bike* to accommodate this new type of bike. Of course, if you had no prior concept of *bike*, anything you read about a bike would be difficult to understand, and you would need to start from the beginning and develop a schema for *bike*.

Good readers assimilate or accommodate what they read into their existing schemata. They sample, predict, confirm, and ultimately integrate the text they read. Why don't poor readers do this?

WHY COMPREHENSION SOMETIMES FAILS TO HAPPEN

There are many reasons some adults and older adolescents have difficulty reading, but one in particular deserves discussion. Poor readers do not understand the *process* of reading because they have not been taught how to read for meaning—they do not view reading as a meaning-making process. Instead, they often feel reading is a *product*—the end result of identifying and sounding out each and every word. Poor readers tend to think that if they correctly call out words, they are reading.

Many learners believe they would be better readers if only they could correctly break down unfamiliar words into phonetic segments. They erroneously equate phonics mastery with reading. Such learners are *phonics-bound*. Others equate the mastery of word identification with reading. These learners are *word-bound*.

Readers who see reading as phonics or word identification have serious problems because they have a mistaken notion of the goal of reading. They need to be taught that reading is a search for meaning, not merely the identification of sounds and words.

Suppose you are learning to play a new board game. Most likely your first question is "What is the object of the game?" Once you understand the object, you can plan your playing strategy. The same is true for reading. Poor readers must learn to understand that the goal of reading is to make sense of print. They need to be encouraged to think before they see, to use their heads in addition to their eyes. Reading is more than a visual activity; it is the process of mentally interacting with text. In short, reading is thinking. An instructor's first task is to help learners understand this.

The following chapters describe specific strategies designed to turn poor readers, who sound out or call out words, into meaning-makers who sample, predict, confirm, and integrate. As you read the strategies and prepare your lessons, ask yourself three questions: "Are my lessons designed to meet the real-world, immediate needs of my student?"; "Am I reinforcing the idea that reading is a meaning-making activity?"; and "Are my lessons consistent with how the process of comprehension happens?" If your answers to these questions are affirmative, your efforts will be rewarded.

CHAPTER

3

Profile One Readers and Teaching Strategies

PROFILE ONE LEARNERS are adults or adolescents who either were in special-education classes as children or would have been placed in such classes had they been available. These learners rarely seek assistance on their own; more often a social service agency or parents initiate enrollment. Once enrolled in an educational program their attendance is generally frequent and consistent. Progress, when present, is painstakingly slow and erratic.

In every remedial reading class and volunteer literacy project, Profile One learners are a reality. In fact, in most ABE programs these learners constitute about 10 percent of the total population served.

While often unable to write or say the alphabet, many Profile One learners can write or "draw" their names. However, sometimes they do not know their own ages, addresses, or birth dates. They have almost no sight vocabulary and their independent and instructional levels are at or below the first grade. Their listening-capacity level is within or even below the second-grade range. Many of these individuals lack the most basic knowledge—one woman told an instructor she had no middle name because she was not married. Another believed paper was made from rocks. Still another stated he was either fifteen or fifty-one years old.

Many individuals who fit this profile may be unable to provide reliable medical histories; but when such information is available, significant instances of severe and sustained childhood illnesses are often revealed. One student missed two years of school because of rheumatic

11

fever; another was blind in one eye from a small cut that became infected and went untreated.

When queried about their concept of print, many Profile One learners cannot respond. They have no concept of what reading is or of why one reads. When able to respond to questions about reading, many of these individuals will describe reading as a process of sounding out words. If sounding out fails, their only other strategy is to ask someone for help.

Over 80 percent of these individuals have vision problems so severe that glasses need to be prescribed before a reliable assessment can continue. One student stated she had glasses; however, when we asked to see those glasses, she produced a pair with shattered lenses. Another man was legally blind; his condition had gone undetected despite enrollment in an ABE center for over two years.

About 70 percent of these learners demonstrate severe auditory discrimination and/or hearing problems; in a small number of cases a hearing aid is actually required. Given these circumstances, attempts to teach phonics will be ineffective. These learners also have a very limited attention span.

The lives of many Profile One learners are marked by significant personal strife. One student was going through a divorce, had received shock treatments for depression, and was a recovering alcoholic. Another, a young woman who had thirteen brothers and sisters all under the age of sixteen, was often on medication for her nerves. She was a victim of child abuse.

Only a small percentage of these individuals are able to live on their own without the assistance of family or a social service agency. Sometimes a former special-education student has elderly, ill parents who are desperately seeking help in fear that after they die, their child will be unable to manage.

The needs of these individuals are evident. The possibility of their ever obtaining even minimal reading skills is remote. In fact, the benefits these learners may derive from tutoring or in an ABE class are questionable.

Anyone working with a Profile One student should have a realistic assessment of his or her learner's abilities. A common problem is that this individual sometimes is placed with a volunteer tutor who is unaware of the learner's very limited potential. Expectations for success are high, only to be shattered when tutoring sessions result in no real progress. Yet well-intentioned tutors are often reluctant to discontinue tutoring such an adult because the learner becomes dependent on him or her. Unfortunately, when this situation occurs, volunteer tutors often become frustrated with themselves. They feel they are to blame for their learners' lack of progress, when this is not necessarily the case. Above all, volunteers should be placed with students who have a reasonable chance to learn to read, a chance not open to most Profile One learners.

If Profile One individuals are placed in classes, instructional time might best be spent working on simple coping skills such as ordering from a menu, using public transportation, and making change instead of attempting to deal with reading, writing, and mathematics. Ideally, they should work with an instructor who has a special-education background. Unfortunately, this is seldom the case.

Of course, it is unthinkable to suggest that Profile One individuals are not worthy of educational efforts and will never make a contribution to society. It must be realized, however, that most of these individuals will never learn to read beyond a few basic sight words and simple sentences.

Susan, whose diagnostic profile follows, is an example of a Profile One adult.

DIAGNOSTIC PROFILE
Name: Susan   *Age: 26*

Background Information

Susan grew up in a small rural town in southern Illinois. She has a speech impediment that makes it difficult to understand her. According to her tutor, she holds a special-education high school diploma. She is a widow with two children, ages four and six, and, until six months ago she held a part-time job cleaning a church. She lost this job because she was unable to obtain reliable transportation.

Susan and her tutor have been working together for five months. They usually meet once a week at the local library. Susan's tutor is somewhat frustrated and concerned because Susan appears to be making no progress.

Reading Ability/View of Reading

Unable to read at all, when asked about reading Susan said she thought she "used to be able to read but forgot how." She was unable to respond to questions such as, "Do you know anyone who is a good reader?" or, "What would you like to be able to read?" It is possible that Susan did not respond because she did not understand the nature of the questions.

When presented with a list of twenty simple words, Susan said she recognized one of them. "I know *i-s*," she said, calling the letters *i* and *s*. When asked what *i-s* spelled, she said she was not sure. It is obvious that Susan had no idea of the nature of reading and no concept of words.

Three short stories at approximately the first-grade reading level were read to Susan. She was asked to retell each story as best she could. Susan was able to do this with only a few problems. When stories at approximately the second-grade level were read to her, however, she was unable to provide adequate retellings.

Susan was able to write her name, though she appeared more to draw it than write it. She was unable to write her address and a bit uncertain about her birth date. Susan knew the days of the week and named eight months of the year—but not in sequential order.

Vision/Auditory Discrimination

When tested for nearsightedness, Susan appeared to have a problem with her left eye. The vision test for farsightedness could not be administered because Susan did not understand or could not remember the test instructions.

Susan failed the auditory discrimination test. She missed eleven of the forty items administered. When an alternate form of the test was administered, she failed ten of forty items. Test results suggested that Susan be given a complete hearing test by an audiologist.

Summary

Susan, a twenty-six-year-old woman, is illiterate. When read to, she is unable to retell stories written above the first-grade level. This low listening level is viewed as Susan's estimated capacity level. That is, at this time Susan can be expected to progress to about the first-grade level. Given Susan's academic background, possible physical limitations (vision and hearing), and the low level (first grade) at which she is able to retell what has been read to her, she is unlikely to make much progress. These concerns should be discussed with Susan's tutor. In addition, Susan should be given complete vision and hearing examinations.

Susan is a typical Profile One learner. Profile One learners often have the following educational characteristics:

Profile One learners—

- Have independent and instructional levels at or below the first-grade range and extremely limited sight vocabulary

- Have listening-capacity levels below the second-grade range, indicating a very low potential to learn

- Were often previously enrolled in special-education classes
- Often have auditory discrimination problems and are unable to repeat short sentences or to express thoughts fluently
- Sometimes have a history of poor and erratic school attendance

The following personal and environmental data were common for Profile One students:

- Sustained childhood illnesses, sometimes accompanied by high fevers
- Often appear in poor health, commonly experience headaches (possibly due to stress), and appear to be hospitalized more frequently than other individuals
- Have chaotic home environments not conducive to studying
- Generally are unemployed or hold very low-skilled jobs

Our intent in describing Profile One learners is to be pragmatic, not pessimistic. Unfortunately, too many instructors and volunteer tutors have been led to hold unrealistic expectations about the progress Profile One learners can make.

TEACHING STRATEGIES FOR PROFILE ONE READERS

1. Reading Interview

Description
The following questions and directions are intended to help you find out what the learner can read and why he or she thinks people read. This activity is an interview with suggestions for discussion, ending with your asking the learner to conduct a brief reading survey. It will help your learner better understand what and why people read. It will also show the learner he or she can indeed read certain things.

Directions

By saying the following set of statements to your learner, he or she may be able to understand that the purpose of reading is to gain meaning.

1. "Tell me everything you have read in the last week." (Try to draw from the learner's everyday experiences to find times when he or she is reading road signs, product labels, store signs, and so on.)

2. "Tell me things you have seen other people read. Why do you think they were reading them?"

3. "Let's list the reasons people read." (To learn something, to follow directions, to be entertained, and so on.)

4. "Let's look at some examples of what people read (candy wrappers, the telephone book, directions for preparing food, and so on) and talk about how we might read each differently because we have a different purpose for reading each one." (Some materials need to be read in their entirety, such as recipes. Other materials require that we read only parts, such as catalogs or the phone book.)

5. "Let's rank and discuss the following in their importance to reading: pronouncing every word correctly, reading aloud smoothly, reading fast, understanding the meaning." (Stress that understanding meaning is the most important.)

6. "During the next week, try to remember what you need to read and why you need to read it. We'll talk about that next week."

7. Have your learner conduct his or her own mini-survey during the week to find out the reasons people read.

Instructional Principle
The poor reader often does not realize how much he or she reads; Profile One learners usually see themselves as completely unable to read when in fact, they often read environmental print such as McDonald's, K-Mart, and "Coca-Cola." Profile One learners often do not know what others read or why they read it. This interview and survey strategy will help Profile One learners see themselves as readers of some words and help them find out what and why other people read.

2. Reading and Beginning Writing

Description
Most Profile One readers are unable to read at all. They need to be read to even before other strategies in this section are used. They need to develop a concept of what reading should sound like, how books are read, and even what words are.

Directions

1. Each session read to the learner and point to the words while you are reading.

2. Ask the learner to point to a word, the beginning of a word, the end of a word, and finally the various letters. If the learner does not know any of these concepts, provide direct instruction.

3. Ask the learner to point to the beginning and end of a page and which way print goes across and down the page. If he or she is confused about any of these concepts, emphasize that we read from left to right and from top to bottom.

4. During each session encourage writing, even if it is no more than scribbling. Ask the learner to read his or her writing.

5. Let the learner watch you write. Read the words as you write them. Grocery lists or "things to do" lists provide a good start; writing post cards or short notes is a helpful second step.

Instructional Principle
A Profile One adult or adolescent needs to be read to just as a child does. However, the stories read should reflect the maturity level and interests of an adult or adolescent. These learners also need to observe how to process print. Remember to *point* to words as you read them to the learner. The concepts of print and of words must be developed as a foundation for reading. Simple writing activities will reinforce the learner's awareness of print.

3. Language-Experience Stories

Description
Language experience is a meaning-making approach to reading that has proved highly successful for many years in helping people learn to read and in helping poor readers improve their reading.

3A. Language-Experience Story Writing

Directions

1. The learner tells you everything he or she knows about something of interest to the learner. List this information on a piece of paper and then go over the list with the learner. The information will become the basis of a story.

2. Write the story on a second sheet of paper word for word as the learner dictates it, saying each word as you write it.

3. When the learner has finished dictating the story, read it back to him or her and ask if there are any changes the learner would like to make.

4. After the desired changes are made, read the story aloud again.

5. Together with the learner, read the story aloud. This step may be repeated several times if necessary.

6. Once the learner feels comfortable with the story, he or she alone reads it aloud. As the learner reads, spot-check for sight vocabulary. Words that give the learner difficulty can be put on sight-word cards for additional practice.

7. Dictate the story into a tape recorder so that the learner can listen to it at home while reading it from the page.

8. Each week the learner can choose spelling words to learn from his or her story. For the next session, type the story, leaving blanks in place of the spelling words. This type of spelling test, which requires the learner to guess the missing words from context, also helps to build reading comprehension.

3B. Language-Experience Stories with Cloze Exercises

Directions

1. After the learner has written several language-experience stories and feels comfortable reading them, select key words from the stories.

2. Replace the key words with blanks for the learner to fill in.

3. Emphasize that the learner can figure out the missing words because he or she already knows the story.

Instructional Principle
The more one knows about a topic and the more meaningful it is to the person, the easier the material will be to read. Even very poor readers are motivated to read their own stories. They know about the topic because it is their own, so lack of background knowledge is not an issue. Recording the story on tape gives the learner a chance to memorize the story. This memorization resembles a stage of reading most beginning readers go through.

4. Environmental Print Book

Description
Prepare a book of words from the learner's immediate environment. A photo album works best for this activity. If one is not available, a spiral notebook or three-ring binder is recommended.

Directions

1. Share with the learner a number of advertisements from a newspaper.

2. Have the learner cut out all the ads that he or she recognizes. Ask your learner to "read" each ad. Then circle the brand names and franchise names in the ads and discuss them.

3. Write each circled word in large letters on an index card.

4. Place the ad on a page of the book with the index card next to or below it.

5. Place several ads and their respective word cards on each page of the book.

6. Review the ad words each time you meet with your learner until he or she identifies them instantly.

Instructional Principle
This book and the language-experience stories become the first reading books for the illiterate adult and adolescent. Most adults and adolescents can recognize many print words from their everyday world in the context of a logo or ad. For example, they often do not read the word *McDonald's* as much as they recognize the golden arch; however, they do know *McDonald's* is a part of that logo. By separating the word *McDonald's* from the entire logo and putting it on a word card, the learner begins to build a sight vocabulary of environmental print words. The goal is to help such learners begin to see themselves as readers.

5. Word Banks

Description
As the learner encounters an important new word, write it on a card. These words become a part of a bank of words that the learner can practice identifying and sorting (once he or she has collected a quantity

of word cards). Words from your learner's language-experience stories and environmental print book are logical words to enter first in this word bank.

5A. Word Bank Identification

Directions

1. Write an important new word on an index card. This word should be one that is somewhat familiar to the learner.

2. On the back of the card, put a picture or any other graphic that would help the learner identify the word.

3. Place this word card in a special place, such as a plastic recipe card holder or a shoe box.

4. Each time you meet with your learner, go over some or all of these cards. This review helps the learner build his or her sight vocabulary.

5. As your learner becomes more familiar with these words, use them as flash cards.

5B. Word Bank Sorting

Directions

1. When the learner has collected at least twenty-five cards in his or her word bank, ask him or her to sort them into categories provided by you. For example, you might want the learner to put all the words starting with *b* in one pile and with *c* in another. Initial consonants can be taught using this procedure.

2. Have the learner sort the words into other categories, such as "thing" words in one pile, "people" words in a second pile, and the rest in a third pile.

3. Develop other categories for your learner to sort. Categories might include things the learner likes or does not like; words associated with food or cars or children; holiday words, sports terms, work words, and so on.

4. Invite your learner to take the pile of words and sort them into his or her own categories. You can make this a game by trying to guess

the category or categories your learner has created. If you can do this activity with a group of learners, you can pair up students and have them exchange their piles of cards and guess each other's "sorts."

Instructional Principle
A word bank consisting of words the learner has encountered while being read to or while trying to read is a far more powerful collection of words than an arbitrary vocabulary list. Building a sight vocabulary is important because it helps the learner feel he or she can read some words without having to sound them out.

Sorting the words gives the instructor a chance to teach initial consonant phonic skills as well as other categorizing skills.

6. Sentence Stems

Description
A sentence stem composed of a subject and a verb is read to the learner. The learner then provides a word or phrase to complete the sentence. The same stem is written over and over again, with the learner providing different words for completion.

6A. Sentence Stem Completion

Directions

1. Choose a two- or three-word stem, such as "I like _____."

2. The learner provides a word that makes sense with this stem, such as *hamburgers*.

3. Write in *hamburgers* and read, "I like hamburgers." Then ask for something else the learner likes and fill in another blank.

4. After you have completed about six "I like" sentences, have the learner practice reading them. If desired, these words can be put into the learner's word bank described in Strategy 5.

5. In future sessions do this strategy with other stems, such as "Work is _____"; "Children are _____"; "I can _____"; "Learning is _____"; "I hate _____"; "Housecleaning is _____."

6B. Alternating Stems

Directions

1. As an alternative to single stems, design two alternating, contrasting stems, such as "I like _____" and "I hate _____," or "I can _____" and "I cannot _____."

2. Ask the learner to fill in the blanks using these alternating stems.

Instructional Principle
Sentence stems provide a high-interest, repetitive sentence structure that gives the learner the opportunity to read with much success. The repeating stem makes that part of the sentence easy to read, and each stem-completing word is provided by the learner. Success in early reading experiences of this type builds an "I can read" attitude in the learner.

7. Predictable Stories

Description
Predictable stories are written with predictable patterns, making the stories easy to read.

Directions

1. Read stories that are highly predictable. There are many commercially produced predictable books.

2. After you read the story, ask the learner to read it back to you. Help the learner until he or she can read the entire story successfully.

3. Make up predictable stories concerning interests of the learner. If a learner is interested in cars, for example, make up a predictable car story. It might read something like this:

   I wanted to see how fast my car would go. By the end of the first block it was going 30 miles per hour. By the end of the second block it was going 40 miles per hour. By the end of the third block it was going 50 miles per hour. . . .

Instructional Principle
A learner is helped tremendously by a predictable text. Because the pattern in the story is repetitive, the learner can figure out the pattern

and read the story successfully. Predictability should be a strong criterion for selecting stories for learners with severe reading disabilities. These stories provide many successful reading experiences.

8. Guessing

Description
When a learner comes to an unfamiliar word, he or she should guess at the word or skip it and come back after finishing the sentence. Guesses should take contextual as well as graphophonic cues into consideration.

Directions

1. When the learner comes to an unfamiliar word, tell him or her to guess at the word.

2. Let the learner read on after the guess without further comment.

3. If the learner will not guess or if the guess was inappropriate, have him or her continue reading the sentence to see if the context will help determine the word.

4. If the word still cannot be identified, ask the learner to go back a line or two and see if the preceding lines suggest the word. If the learner still does not guess a word, ask him or her to read the sentence once again until a good guess is made.

5. Ask the learner to reread the sentence. Provide the initial consonant sound of the word and ask the learner to try to guess again.

6. Provide oral examples in which the learner uses the information provided to anticipate the missing word. (For example: "The dog was chewing on a _____." "Apples grow on _____." "The baby began to _____.")

Instructional Principle
Profile One readers are usually very low risk takers. They often stop reading when they come to an unknown word and try to sound it out. But by taking the time to do this, they forget what they have already read, and meaning is lost. Because some stop to sound out two or three words in every sentence, they lose all sense of what they are reading.

A learner should be encouraged to guess at unfamiliar words or to skip them and then go back rather than try to sound them out. As a last resort, if a guess is inaccurate and the context is of little help, the learner can go back to the word and either sound it out or simply be provided with the word.

9. Nonsense-Word Substitutions

Description
If the learner produces a nonsense word or omits unfamiliar words, help him or her realize that reading is a meaningful process and that words pronounced should make sense. In short, reading should sound like oral language.

Directions

1. Ask the learner what his or her nonsense word means. It is possible that the learner knows its meaning but has mispronounced the word.

2. Provide oral and written examples for which the learner must attempt to guess the word that has been omitted. (For example: "I will mail the _____." "The dog _____ over the fence.")

3. Provide examples that contain nonsense words and ask the learner to tell what the nonsense words might mean. (For example: "He drank a glass of *fax*." "The *zop* bought some candy.")

4. If the learner omits an unfamiliar word, ask questions such as these:
   Does that make sense?
   Does that sound like language to you?
   What word do you think could go in this spot?
   Why do you think so?
   What word do you know that begins like ___ but would make sense?

5. If the learner is unable to produce a word with the same beginning sound, ask him or her to try a word that *would* make sense. The goal is to have the reader produce a word or a nonword rather than omitting a word. Remember, though, that there are times when a word can be omitted without a loss of meaning.

Instructional Principle
Profile One readers usually think that calling out words is more important than making meaning. They overuse phonic cues and underuse context cues. Substituting nonsense words forces readers to *think* in order to determine unfamiliar words.

10. Sounding Out

Description
By providing only initial letters of words in context, you can show Profile

One readers that meaning should be considered before any attempt is made to sound out a word.

Directions

1. Prepare short sentences. The first word of each should begin with a consonant. Provide only the first letter or letters of the first word, followed by cue words.

    Cl_____ the door.

    P_____ the butter.

    Dr_____ your coffee.

    Point out that if one reads to the end of a sentence, the unknown word can often be determined, even though only the initial letter or letters are provided.

2. End a short sentence with a blank.

    We wash our fa_____.

    We wash our ha_____.

    Point out that if one makes sense of the first part of the sentence, the initial letter or letters are all that is needed to provide the unknown word.

Instructional Principle
If meaning is stressed, the initial letter or letters of a word will often provide the necessary information to identify the word. Phonic instruction for the Profile One reader, therefore, should focus on initial letters. This activity should always be done in the context of sentences.

CHAPTER

4

Profile Two Readers
and Teaching Strategies

THE READING ABILITIES of Profile Two learners differ from those of Profile One in a critical way. Profile Two learners, whose independent and instructional levels range from pre-first to about mid-first grade, have a listening-capacity level within the mid-fifth- to mid-seventh-grade range. This level indicates that these learners have the language skills necessary for them to learn to read newspapers, job application forms, and other practical materials. Unlike most Profile One students, Profile Two learners generally have well-developed oral language skills.

Although over half the learners in this profile have been in special-education classes, they appear to have devised coping skills that enable them to mask their low literacy skills and obtain steady employment. Frequently, these individuals appear to have fallen through the cracks in the educational system. One Profile Two learner attended fourteen elementary schools in eight years. Another attended three different schools (in the same town) during first grade. One woman became pregnant when she was in fifth grade; she quit school, moved to another city to live with her older sister, and never attended school again. Unlike Profile One students, Profile Two learners are more often in formal educational programs than in a volunteer setting.

Over 80 percent of the learners in Profile Two view reading as a process of sounding out parts of words or memorizing individual words. Unlike Profile One individuals, all these learners have some sense of print and reading; however, they rarely make a connection between reading and meaning.

Like Profile One learners, many Profile Two individuals have significant vision problems. Almost 70 percent need glasses or wear outdated prescriptions. In addition, 40 percent have auditory discrimination problems.

Profile Two learners, like many individuals with reading disabilities, talk of significant instances of childhood strife. For instance, two adult learners had been raised by three sets of foster parents before they were in third grade. Other learners found it necessary to interrupt their schooling to raise brothers and sisters or to work to support large families. Poor diets as children, interrupted education, and family problems appear to be the chief reasons these learners failed to achieve as children. If some of the environmental drawbacks had been removed in their earlier years, these learners would likely have become functionally literate.

The outlook for students with this profile is optimistic. With proper instruction and perseverance, these learners have the potential to become readers. Because perseverance is critical when teaching Profile Two readers, you might want to review the Conversation Suggestions offered in Chapter 1, paying special attention to the fact that lapses are to be expected. Leo, whose diagnostic profile follows, is a typical Profile Two learner.

DIAGNOSTIC PROFILE

Name: Leo   *Age: 31*

Background Information

Leo grew up in a rural Arkansas community. He is one of twenty-one brothers and sisters, all children of the same mother and father. His family was poor, and because Leo was one of the older children, he often stayed home from school to work or to help his mother.

At age thirteen, Leo and a younger brother left Arkansas and moved to Chicago to live with a sister and attend a trade school. Unaccustomed to large cities and urban life, Leo and his brother were ridiculed by their classmates for their clothing, speech, and mannerisms.

While attending the trade school, Leo majored in carpentry and mechanics. He quit school when he was sixteen and moved to the St. Louis area to help a younger sister who was very ill. In St. Louis he first worked on highway construction, then in a gas station. He currently is unemployed and is seeking job training.

Reading Ability/View of Reading

Leo's independent level does not appear to be beyond that of pre-first grade. His instructional level is estimated to be in the pre-first-grade to low-first-grade range. In contrast, when short stories were read to Leo, he was able to listen and adequately retell them at about the seventh-grade level.

Leo misunderstands the reading process. He views it as learning to read isolated words. This overdependence on words alone caused him to lose meaning when he read short passages. In a passage of fifty words, Leo misread almost half yet made no self-corrections. For example, he read, "It was filled" for "It was fall" and "Why was trees" for "They saw trees." Because Leo had no idea that reading should make sense, he read nonsensically.

When queried about the strategies he used or might use as a reader, Leo said that the most important part of reading is to "know words." According to Leo, his former teachers would test his spelling to help him learn to read. Leo did not understand that reading is a process of gaining meaning from print. He mistakenly thought that mastery of individual words leads to understanding.

Vision/Auditory Discrimination

Although Leo passed the auditory discrimination test, he had problems on the tests for farsightedness and nearsightedness. Two weeks later he passed these tests proudly wearing new glasses donated by a local Lions Club.

Summary

Leo can read very little by himself. The causes of his problems appear to be largely environmental, and his main problem seems to be his lack of understanding that reading is a meaning-making process. Based upon his listening-capacity level, Leo appears to have the potential to improve a great deal. With his new glasses, he has no vision problems. Leo would benefit a great deal from instruction with a literacy tutor or in an ABE program. If enrolled in a classroom setting, he will need a great deal of individual attention.

Leo is a typical Profile Two learner. These individuals do have the potential to learn to read. Profile Two adults are characterized by the following educational factors:

Profile Two learners—

- Have independent and instructional levels below the second-grade range

- Have listening-capacity levels ranging from mid-fifth to mid-seventh grade

- May have been in special education but have developed adequate coping strategies

Profile Two learners are characterized by the following personal and environmental traits:

- Generally have a history of employment even if they are not currently employed

- Usually have a history of interrupted schooling

- Often experienced extended illnesses when young

- Grew up with a great deal of family trauma

It is important to remember that Profile Two learners have the potential to learn to read. With proper instructional strategies they will achieve that goal.

TEACHING STRATEGIES FOR PROFILE TWO READERS

Recommended strategies for Profile Two learners include the teaching strategies given for Profile One learners if you feel they are appropriate, as well as new ones, which follow:

11. Good Reader Strategies

Description
The following "Good Reader Strategies" adapted from an article by Cooper and Petrosky (1976), should be reviewed during at least six of the teaching or tutoring sessions. These strategies explain the tactics that good readers use—tactics that poor readers often do not know. The strategies will help break the disabling notion that reading is a sounding-out or word-calling process and will strengthen the notion that it is meaning-making.

Good readers are active readers. Good readers bring their own knowledge of the world to the material they are reading. The case study that follows is an example of a reader's failure to do so.

A tutor selected an article for an adult disabled reader because of the reader's interest in snakes. The title of the article was "Snakes in Your Own Backyard." The learner started to read the title by sounding out the word *snake*. He began by saying the *s* sound, then *sn*, and so on. The tutor asked him what he thought a word starting with *sn* in the title of an article about snakes might be. He replied, "Oh, snakes."

They then talked about "using your head" as well as your eyes while reading. The tutor explained that reading is done by thinking and predicting, not just by seeing. The print on the page is the starting place; it gives the brain information to process. Often a reader does not have to sound out a word because he or she can actually figure it out with very little visual (print) information.

The tutor then asked the learner to guess what a long word starting with *rat* might be in an article about snakes. The learner replied that it might be *rattlesnake*. Later, as he read the article, he identified the word *rattlesnake* immediately.

That example illustrates the need to talk to the learner about using his or her head—about bringing prior knowledge to the page and using that knowledge to think and predict. Print is far easier to understand if the reader is ahead of his or her own eyes, predicting what comes n _ _ _.

Good readers take chances.   Good readers risk being wrong in order to gain more meaning. One of the major problems poor readers have is that they are not risk takers. They are anxious about reading and often stumble over every word that is not immediately recognizable. Their reading becomes slow and laborious, and they lose comprehension.

These readers must be encouraged to take chances—to increase speed and guess at meaning—so that comprehension is possible. Be willing to spend plenty of time assuring the reader that it is all right to make guesses when reading. Simple activities unrelated to reading can help get this point across. For example, having the learner guess what is in a wallet or purse will encourage him or her to understand the concept of risk taking.

Good readers guess at or just skip words they are not sure of.   This rule is closely related to the previous one. If you have encouraged a learner to take chances, he or she will more likely feel comfortable guessing at or skipping unfamiliar words. Suppose, for example, a learner is reading the sentence "The man used his microwave to heat up the food" and stops at the word *microwave* because it is a long word that is not in his or her sight vocabulary. Simply ask the learner to guess at the word or skip it if no guess is made. Above all, encourage the learner to continue reading. Initially, continuing is difficult for the poor reader because he or she feels it is cheating to guess at a word or skip it. Such learners feel it is necessary to stop to sound out each unfamiliar word. Continue to encourage your learner to take chances with, guess at, and skip words.

In the sentence about the microwave, the reader has some information to make a guess about the word. The reader knows that it is a "man" who is "using" something. This information is probably not enough to make a guess at something a man uses that starts with *mic*. Here is where the importance of reading ahead must be stressed. The information that this unfamiliar word was something a man used to "heat up food" can then be used to help the reader guess the word. This process gives the reader a great deal of information to determine the word. It reduces drastically the number of alternatives he or she has to deal with in attacking it. If the reader has any experience with microwave ovens, he or she should have little difficulty figuring out that the word is *microwave*. If the reader has no experience with microwave ovens, the word should be read to him or her and explained.

Suppose the reader stopped when first reading the sentence and tried to sound out the word *microwave*. The result might have sounded something like this: "mi," "mic," "mic-ro," "mic-ro-wa," "mic-ro-wa, wave." The process of sounding out places too much emphasis on individual sounds and word identification at the expense of meaning.

The reader who skipped the word to obtain help from the rest of the sentence has much more information to determine the unfamiliar word. In fact, this reader will probably guess "microwave" after going back and looking at the beginning of the word. The letter *m* or *mic* would alert him or her that the word is *microwave*. Encourage the use of context—many times the initial consonant or syllable is all that remains necessary to determine an unfamiliar word.

Good readers read as though they expect the material to make sense. The best way to understand very difficult or unfamiliar material is to read on and expect the material to make sense.

All good readers have had the experience of reading a text, perhaps on an involved subject such as physics or philosophy, and discovering that their limited prior knowledge makes the text difficult to understand. When faced with this problem, good readers read through the material to find something they *can* understand. They then reread and build on that information to make sense of the text. Good readers continue building by rereading the difficult text, each time gaining new knowledge.

Poor readers must be encouraged to do the same thing—to read through the text and look for something that is understandable. They should then be told to reread the text, attaching information to what they do understand. Some of the text will make sense the first time; more will be understood by rereading, and further meaning will result with each new reading. Too often, disabled readers immediately give up when they have difficulty with a text. If they are taught how to build meaning by rereading, they will start to expect material to make sense.

Good readers try not to read too slowly. Because poor readers read so slowly, they often forget what they have read by the time they reach the end of the sentence or paragraph. The/y/ ha/ve/ bro/k/en/ the/ sen/ten/ce/ in/to/ su/ch/ sm/all/ bit/s/ th/at/ the/y/ ha/ve/ lo/st/ it/ all. By skipping words, reading on, and guessing, they will not interrupt the flow of their reading and can use their heads to gain meaning rather than attend to individual sounds and words.

Good readers change their approach depending on the purpose of their reading. Often, poor readers believe it is necessary to read each and every word, regardless of what they are reading. Because of this, they complain that reading is too hard and takes too long.

To combat this reaction, instructors should discuss their own reading experiences. Explain, for example, that you read a new and complicated recipe in a different manner from the way you read a birthday card. Preparing tax returns requires reading for detail, while reading a short magazine article usually does not. The learner needs to know that people change their approach depending upon how much they already know about the subject and upon their purpose for reading.

Prior knowledge affects the way a good reader reads. For example, an experienced coin collector might skim an article about coin collecting, while the novice collector would read it very carefully. It is important to share these experiences with a learner. Remind the learner to determine how much he or she already knows about a topic before determining how to approach the reading.

Why someone chooses to read something also directly influences the way in which the person reads. Explain to the learner, for example, that if you want to change an electrical outlet receptacle in your wall, you do not have to read an entire home repair book. You need only locate the chapter about electricity and read the section on electrical outlets. Conversely, if you are preparing a special dish for the first time, you need to read the entire recipe carefully and refer to it over and over again as you prepare the dish.

Directions

1. Put each of the Good Reader Strategies on an index card.

2. Introduce and discuss one or two of the strategies each session.

3. During each session review the strategies that have already been discussed.

4. Ask the learner to list the Good Reader Strategies and explain them during each session until all are learned and understood.

5. Whenever possible, connect the teaching strategy you are using to an appropriate Good Reader Strategy.

6. Give as many specific examples as you can to illustrate each Good Reader Strategy.

7. A note of caution: Many learners will be able to list the strategies and discuss them relatively easily. Integrating them, however, takes time. To actually *use* these strategies when reading, a learner will need two or three months of constant instruction and reminders.

Instructional Principle

The Good Reader Strategies are the foundation for developing in poor readers a better understanding of the reading process. These strategies provide a new understanding of reading and form the basis for changing phonics-bound or word-bound readers into meaning-makers. Many of the strategies presented in this book can and should be related to one or more of these Good Reader Strategies.

12. Silly Sentences

Description

This strategy forces the learner to read for meaning to understand the use of an inappropriate word.

Directions

1. Make up a sentence in which one word is silly and does not make sense. (For example: "I smell with my knees." "I ate my belt.")

2. Have the learner figure out which word is silly.

3. Make up additional sentences containing silly words.

4. Invite the learner to make up his own silly sentences.

5. Stress that good readers always try to make sense out of what they read.

Instructional Principle

This strategy places emphasis on the whole sentence rather than individual words. The entire sentence must be read with meaning to determine which word is silly.

13. Written Conversation

Description

Written conversation is an enjoyable reading and writing activity for Profile Two readers. It is a version of the language-experience approach and was developed by Carolyn Burke (1985). Instead of talking out loud about something, you and the learner write a conversation. The topic might be a specific event you both know about, such as a bad thunderstorm; your feelings about home or children; or something as simple as what the two of you have done since your last session together.

Directions

1. Start a conversation by briefly writing down what you want to say about the topic selected.

2. Hand the sheet of paper to the learner who reads the comment and responds with one of his or her own.

3. The learner hands the sheet back to you. This process continues until the two of you have no more to say during the time or space allotted.

4. Take a few minutes to discuss orally what has been written.

5. Encourage the learner to write even if you cannot read his or her writing. However, after the learner has finished writing, ask him or her to read it aloud. Then you can respond in writing.

6. If the learner cannot read your writing, read it aloud, pointing to the words so the learner can follow along.

Instructional Principle

Written conversation connects reading and writing and helps develop fluency in both. It reduces the threat and increases the interest in both reading and writing. It also reinforces the partially correct adage that reading is "speech written down."

14. Flash-card Directions

Description

This flash-card activity forces the Profile Two word callers to read more than one word at a time.

Directions

1. On an index card, write a direction of five to ten words, such as "Put your hands on the table" or "Please sit down on the chair."

2. Flash each card and ask the learner to do what the card says. Often the learner will read only the first few words. Encourage "chunking," or grouping words in one glance.

3. Flash the card again and explain that the learner must read ahead and look at all the words. It may take four or five flashes for the learner to understand and do what is directed on the card.

4. Each time you flash a card, urge the learner to skip the words already read and read the next words. (A poor reader tends to start over no matter how many times he or she has read it.)

5. After the reader has mastered a one-direction flash card, prepare cards with two or more directions, such as "Pick up the book and turn to page 10."

Instructional Principle
Often, poor readers start at the beginning of a passage and slowly read every word, no matter what their purpose for reading may be. Flash-card directions require them to read quickly what they already know and read carefully only that which they do not know.

15. Prime-O-Tec (Primary Oral Technique)

Description
Prime-O-Tec (Jordan 1967) is a read-along activity in which the learner reads along with a story that you have previously taped. This activity requires a tape recorder and large headphones. The learner chooses the material he or she wishes to have taped, even though it may be above his or her current reading level. The goal is to build sight vocabulary by capitalizing upon the learner's interests and listening skills.

Directions

1. Record the selected story, reading at a slightly slower than normal rate. Passages of 150 to 300 words are recommended.

2. Using large headphones to block out all other noise, the learner listens to the tape and follows along in the book, moving his or her finger under each word. Watch to make sure the learner is listening and moving his or her finger in synchronization with the tape.

3. After listening to the story a few times, the learner reads aloud with your taped voice, again moving his or her finger under the words while reading. If the learner does not know a word, he or she should say it immediately after your voice on the tape does.

4. After the learner has read the taped material several times and feels

comfortable with the story, he or she should read it aloud to you without the tape. Note any problems. The goal is to read orally with 95 percent accuracy. Words miscalled that do not change the meaning should not be counted as errors.

5. After the learner has read the passage, randomly point to individual words to make sure he or she has not simply memorized the story. The goal is to build vocabulary.

6. In the beginning, each short story or article may require forty-five minutes to one hour of practice. This practice time will decrease rapidly (to about thirty minutes) after three or four sessions.

7. The learner should take the story (or several stories) and the tape home and listen to it over and over again.

Instructional Principle

Profile Two readers usually do not read because they feel it is too difficult. By modeling good reading and building sight vocabulary, this activity aims at making reading for these learners less difficult because it allows interest and listening skills to compensate for low independent reading ability. The learner is able to read materials that, using other approaches, he or she may not have been able to read. Prime-O-Tec uses the learner's strength in oral language to fortify his or her weakness in written language.

This activity is excellent for individuals who can read very little independently because it provides material for independent practice. Any reading material—magazines, short stories, newspapers, and so on—may be taped. Always stress to learners that good readers read a lot and that one becomes a better reader by practicing reading.

16. Card Chunking

Description
This strategy is a categorization activity. The learner groups three words into one meaningful, general concept.

Directions

1. On one side of an index card, write the names of three items that fall into one category (for example, match, smoke, hot = fire; bat, mitt, bases = baseball; thread, needle, cloth = sewing). On the other side of the card, write the name of the category.

2. Ask the learner to read the sides of the cards with the three items and categorize them.

3. After the learner has categorized at his or her own pace with five or six cards, start flashing new cards. Increase the speed so that the learner must read all three words to be categorized at once.

4. Make a game out of it and time how fast the learner can categorize.

5. Invite the learner to write several of his or her own cards with words and categories. See if you can determine the categories.

Instructional Principle
This activity is intended to help the Profile Two reader chunk words into meaningful, general concepts rather than reading every word as a separate, specific unit.

Stress that good readers relate words and ideas.

17. Sentence Chunking

Description
Sentence chunking is another strategy that requires the word-by-word reader to chunk words into meaningful groups.

Directions

1. Provide a list of words such as the one below and ask the learner to create as many sentences as possible from the list.

Mary	old	six
years	young	skated
house	home	friend's
from	only	her

2. Encourage the learner to build increasingly more complex sentences, such as those below.

Mary skated.
Mary skated home.
Mary skated home from her friend's house.
Young Mary skated home from her friend's house.
Young Mary, only six years old, skated home from her friend's house.

Instructional Principle
Although good readers chunk words into meaningful units, word-by-word readers often do not. Sentence chunking helps them develop this skill.

18. Simple Predicting

Description

The following activities require the learner to make simple, obvious predictions. They begin by giving the learner an object or a situation that will allow him or her to make a sensible prediction and later confirm it.

18A. Wallet Predicting

Directions

1. Place a wallet or purse in front of the learner.

2. Ask the learner to guess what is in the wallet or purse.

3. Let the learner find out how many of the guesses were correct.

18B. Number Predicting

Directions

1. Prepare index cards with easily predicted patterns, such as 2, 4, __, 8, 10 . . . or . . . a b __ d e __ g h.

2. Make the patterns increasingly more difficult.

3. Help the learner figure out the pattern.

18C. Prepared-Story Predicting

Directions

1. With input from the learner, write a simple short story with the learner as the main character. You might take a headline from a newspaper and insert the learner's name into the headline. (For example, change the headline "Clark Hits Home Run to Win Game" to "John Smith Hits Home Run to Win Game.")

2. Have the learner read each paragraph of the story after the two of you have written it with his or her name inserted.

3. Ask the learner to predict what is going to happen next.

4. If the learner finds the story too difficult to read independently, read the passage out loud, but still ask him or her to make predictions after each paragraph.

Instructional Principle
As noted earlier, good readers are always guessing and predicting, almost unconsciously, while poor readers are low risk-takers who seldom predict. The strategies above help them realize how using their heads can help them become better readers.

19. Comic-Strip Sequencing

Description
Comic-strip sequencing requires the reader to make sense of a short story line by putting the frames of a comic strip into their correct order.

Directions

1. Take a simple newspaper comic strip of three to five frames and cut each frame out.

2. Paste or tape each frame to an index card, then mix the cards up.

3. Let the learner look at the pictures and read the text first; then ask him or her to put the frames of the comic strip in order.

4. Ask the learner to explain why he or she arranged the frames in that order.

5. Talk about why the learner was right or wrong and how to go about figuring the right order. Stress the idea that reading is figuring out how words and sentences relate to each other; it is not simply identifying separate words. Reinforce the idea that the reader must think as well as see.

Instructional Principle
Poor readers who read word by word often have trouble relating the words within sentences or the sentences themselves together. This strategy requires the learner to relate words and sentences to one another. The picture clues help the reader make sense of the words and sentences so that discovering meaning is more easily done than in other reading activities.

20. Riddles

Description
Profile Two learners like to figure out riddles, so this activity should be fun and of high interest. You can use riddles from books or make up your own.

Directions

1. Prepare or select a riddle such as the following:
    I have feathers.
    I can fly.
    I sing.
    What am I?

2. Have the learner read the first line while you cover up the other lines.

3. Ask the learner to write down what he or she thinks is described in the first line.

4. Reveal the second line. Allow the learner to modify his or her prediction if necessary.

5. Reveal the third line and again have the learner confirm or change his or her prediction.

6. Continue until you reach the end of the riddle.

    Here's a variation. Instead of ending with "What am I?" end with "Who am I?" or "Where am I?" The following is an example of a longer and more difficult riddle.

    You need me and so does everyone.
    I am very useful.
    You cannot get along without me.
    Some days you can see me clearly.
    Other days you cannot.
    But I am always there.
    Without me you would not live.
    The world would be in darkness.
    I provide the earth with light.
    What am I? (The sun)

Instructional Principle
Meaning is woven together as one reads from sentence to sentence. The reader predicts, reads on to confirm, and changes predictions as neces-

sary. Riddles help emphasize the predicting and confirming nature of reading.

21. Incomplete Sentences

Description
This activity uses a very simple version of the cloze procedure, a fill-in-the-blank activity. Selective blank spaces are placed in a text.

Directions

1. Prepare a series of high-interest sentences, each with a word deleted. For example:

   John takes out his key.
   John puts his key in the (____). (door)
   John opens the (____). (door)
   John turns on the (____). (light)

2. Ask the learner to guess what word goes in the first blank. If he or she will not make a guess, move on to the remaining lines. Discuss the words in the sentences that are clue words.

3. If the learner makes a guess, ask why he or she chose that particular word.

Instructional Principle
Poor readers often fail to look at sentence context clues to help them. This word-deletion activity forces the learner to attend to context clues.

22. Meaningful Substitutions

Description
As a learner is reading orally, he or she may substitute words that make sense. In such cases, remain silent. Correct only those substitutions that do not make sense or that alter the meaning.

Directions
To help the learner decide which substitutions make sense, try the strategies that follow.

1. Provide sentences containing a substituted word written above the text. Read the sentence and then discuss whether the substituted

word made sense. (For example, "They went to the zoo because there (they) were many things to see.")

2. Provide exercises that contain sentences with substitutions made by two different readers. Discuss which substitution appears to be closer to the author's intended meaning. (For example, "Bill decided to take the (a) bus to work" and "Bill decided to take (talk) the bus to work.")

Instructional Principle
Searching for meaning is the core of reading. Substitutions that do not affect meaning should be ignored. Stopping a learner to correct every miscalled word only reinforces his or her disabling misconception of reading.

CHAPTER
5

Profile Three Readers and Teaching Strategies

ALTHOUGH BETTER READERS than those previously discussed, Profile Three readers appear to be much like Profile Two learners with two exceptions: Their current ability levels are much higher, and they generally improve at a much faster pace. Indeed, they are able to read some things by themselves. These learners usually have independent levels in the second-grade range and instructional levels from low third to low fourth grade. Listening-capacity levels vary from low sixth grade to mid-seventh grade; this range indicates the potential to become proficient readers.

Profile Three readers have one major problem that is the cause of their reading disabilities. As with Profile One and Two learners, they misunderstand the goal of reading. Almost half the learners in this group believe that reading is "sounding out words." These learners are *phonics-bound*. Another one-third of the Profile Three learners believe reading is a process "of learning a lot of words" and of studying vocabulary; these learners are *word-bound*. Francis told us, "I'll know I'm a good reader when I can read and understand *every* word."

Often, Profile Three learners view dictionary skills as synonymous with reading. One learner in this profile referred to her dictionary six times while reading a passage of 250 words (she kept interrupting herself!). Knowing how to use the dictionary *is* useful, but overdependence on a dictionary breaks one's pattern of thought and disrupts comprehension.

An instructor's main task with Profile Three learners is to help them see that relying exclusively on phonics is not helpful. *Meaning* must be stressed first and foremost.

Many of the learners in this profile (about 60 percent) have vision problems. However, once tested, they also have the initiative to contact a vision specialist themselves and obtain prescription glasses. Over one-third of the learners in Profile Three have acute auditory discrimination problems.

Profile Three learners have relatively few instances of specific language disabilities. Like Profile Two readers, they have devised ingenious coping skills to hide their language and reading problems. One man, for example, worked for a barge company and was responsible for recording what was loaded on and off several boats. To record the loading, he used a small tape recorder; each night he would play the tapes for his wife while she wrote the required information on company forms. Frustrated over the necessity to continually rely on others for help, this Profile Three learner and others like him eventually decide to improve their reading skills.

David, whose report follows, is an example of a Profile Three learner.

DIAGNOSTIC PROFILE
Name: David   *Age: 18*

Background Information

David was referred for testing by his ABE teacher, who noticed he was having difficulty keeping up with the demands of the class. David stated that he would like to be a welder and took training in a vocational school. His main goal is to read well enough to interpret blueprints. David realizes that he has reading and spelling problems and sincerely wants to improve his reading.

Reading Ability/View of Reading

David's independent level is within the second-grade range. He can read some comic strips, the headlines of tabloids such as the *National Enquirer* and the *Star*, and some of his seven-year-old niece's schoolbooks. His instructional level is within the mid-third grade range. With assistance, he is able to read some of the lowest-level textbooks in his reading class. David's listening-capacity level is approximately upper sixth grade.

When reading orally, he reads in a slow, monotonous manner. He miscalls words but generally is able to correct them. When David encounters a word he does not know, he often stops and spells the word, as though spelling it will help him pronounce it. If this strategy fails, he asks to be told the word. He can neither use context clues nor monitor his own comprehension.

When asked about his views of reading and his past experiences in learning to read, David stated that his elementary teachers often asked him to practice reading out loud. He remembers reading passages over and over again to get every word correct. When questioned about the meaning of what he was reading, David said, "Pronouncing it right comes first. That's the most important thing." If David were to teach someone to read, he said he would have them practice the words they did not know.

This excessive attention to the mastery of individual words and a great deal of anxiety about correct pronunciation appears to be the cause of David's problem. That is, he is paying so much attention to each word that his brain is unable to focus on comprehension.

Vision/Auditory Discrimination

A vision screening revealed nearsightedness in both eyes. David said he often caught himself squinting if he had to read the blackboard. Driving and watching television were also beginning to give him problems.

David also appeared to have a mild auditory discrimination problem, with medial vowel sounds causing him the most problems.

Summary

Although David's independent and instructional levels range from second to mid-third grade, his listening-capacity level is approximately sixth grade. The main cause of his reading problem appears to be overdependence upon mastery of words at the expense of comprehension. All instructional sessions should focus upon the concept that reading is an activity designed to gain meaning from print, not to simply pronounce print. Because of his auditory discrimination problem, phonics instruction, particularly with vowel sounds, will probably not be helpful. It is also recommended he see a vision specialist to explore his nearsightedness further.

With proper guidance, David is expected to improve his reading rapidly.

David is a typical Profile Three learner. Profile Three learners are characterized by the educational traits that follow.

Profile Three learners—

- Have independent levels that range from second to third grade and instructional levels from low third to low fourth grade

- Have a listening-capacity level three to four years above their independent level, ranging from low sixth to mid-seventh grade

- Misunderstand the nature of reading. These learners believe reading is a system of mastering sounds or memorizing vocabulary. They feel if they discover the proper "system," they will become good readers. This misunderstanding regarding the nature of reading is their major problem. Attention must be focused upon meaning.

- Usually have completed nine years of school

Profile Three learners are characterized by the following environmental and personal data:

- Are usually in a stable home environment

- Have a history of part time or full-time employment but in occupations requiring only minimal reading skills

- Are highly motivated and persistent learners

As with Profile Two learners, the outlook for Profile Three learners is optimistic. With proper instruction, these individuals will improve greatly.

TEACHING STRATEGIES FOR PROFILE THREE READERS

In addition to the new strategies explained in this chapter, the Good Reader Strategies listed below are helpful to use with Profile Three learners. (These strategies and a method for teaching them were explained in Chapter 4.)

Good readers are active readers.

Good readers take chances.

Good readers guess at words.

Good readers read as though they expect the material to make sense.

Good readers try not to read too slowly.

Good readers change their approach depending upon the material they are reading.

Teach and review the Good Reader Strategies to the Profile Three learner during each session.

23. List It and Skip It Bookmark

Description
This strategy uses a bookmark to encourage the learner to read on rather than stop to sound out unfamiliar words.

Directions

1. Make a bookmark with construction paper or similar material.

2. Write the sentence "List It and Skip It" at the top of the bookmark.

3. Explain that the sentence will remind the learner what to do when he or she is reading and comes to an unfamiliar word.

4. Ask the learner to use the bookmark to jot down any unfamiliar word he or she encounters. Once the word is listed, the learner should simply go on reading.

5. When the learner has finished reading, ask him or her to cross out any words on the list that he or she has already figured out by reading on.

6. Help the learner figure out the meaning of words not crossed out. Context clues, the dictionary, and sounding-out strategies can be used at this time.

7. Ask the learner which of the words on the list he or she feels would be important to know. Discuss which words will likely be encountered again. Note the words the learner selects and use them as part of sight-vocabulary instruction.

Instructional Principle
The bookmark strategy helps the phonics-bound reader, who stops often to attack words and thus loses the meaning of sentences and even whole passages. Point out that some words are not necessary to know because meaning can be determined without them. Often meaning can be discovered by simply reading on and using context.

24. Phrase Chunking and Key Word Identification

Description
The following chunking strategy can decrease the number of times a learner's eyes stop while reading and, at the same time, increase his or her eye span and speed. It will also help the learner locate key words—those words that carry the meaning of sentences.

Directions

1. Divide a sentence into phrases with lines separating the phrases, like this: Divide a sentence / into phrases / with lines separating / the phrases. Each phrase should be a meaningful unit, such as a prepositional phrase or a noun phrase. Most of the phrases will be two or three words long.

2. Explain that the learner need only read the most important word in each phrase to understand it. Demonstrate this idea by picking out the most important word in each marked phrase. Underline or circle the key words you select.

3. Ask the learner to try this activity and pick out the most important word in each phrase.

4. Prepare a story with only the important words in each phrase included. Leave blanks where the deleted words would be.

5. Invite the learner to read the story and tell you about it.

6. Provide another copy of the story with all the words. Ask the learner to read the story again.

7. Discuss what can be learned from the complete version versus the skeleton version. In most instances, the two stories will not be that much different.

8. Emphasize that chunking words into phrases helps highlight the key words that carry the meaning.

Instructional Principle
Key words in each phrase can carry the meaning of a sentence. Profile Three readers, who laboriously process each word, should be made aware of this. Locating key words will help readers break away from word calling and give them practice chunking sentences into meaningful units.

25. Model Reading

Description
Model reading is a strategy used to increase reading speed. It is helpful for learners who read so slowly and deliberately that they often lose the meaning of a sentence or passage because they take so long to reach the end of it. Model reading allows you to show learners how a good reader can read quickly with comprehension.

25A. Alternate Reading

Directions

1. Quickly read out loud a phrase in a sentence—a prepositional phrase, a noun clause, a verb phrase, and so on—and stop.

2. Direct the learner to begin reading immediately, starting at the point where you stopped. The learner should read only the next phrase, as quickly as you read.

3. Jump in, interrupting the learner at the end of his or her phrase. Read the next phrase and stop.

4. Alternate reading thus. Control the pace as well as the stopping and starting points in the text.

5. Require the learner to speed up to match your reading rate. Make it a challenge and a game.

25B. Echo Reading

Directions

1. Instead of you and the learner alternating reading, you may want the learner to read along with you at the pace you dictate. This echo reading will speed up the oral reading of the learner and increase his or her fluency.

2. Begin with passages no longer than 150 to 200 words.

Instructional Principle
Misconception of the goal of reading and anxiety about their ability to read cause many readers to read too slowly. The intent of this strategy is to break the learner's habit of reading slowly and therefore inefficiently.

26. Predicting and Confirming

Description
This strategy encourages the learner to make predictions as he or she is reading. It helps the learner read purposefully to determine whether his or her predictions were right.

Directions

1. Select an interesting story and ask the learner to read the title and look at any pictures accompanying the text.

2. Ask the learner to predict what he or she thinks the story is going to be about. Write the predictions on an index card or a sheet of paper.

3. Ask the learner to read the first few paragraphs (or the first page) to see whether his or her predictions are right. Stop and return to the predictions.

4. If the predictions were on the right track, compliment the learner and have him or her make further predictions about the next section.

5. If the predictions were incorrect, discuss why that might be so. Then have the learner make new predictions about the next paragraph, the next section, or the next page.

6. Have the learner go through the entire story, stopping at logical places to confirm predictions. Incorrect predictions can be crossed out. Correct ones can be circled or checked. Always ask the learner to make new predictions before continuing.

Instructional Principle
Profile Three learners place too much emphasis on the visual aspect of decoding print rather than making meaning. The Predicting and Confirming strategy reinforces the concept that reading is a thinking activity. Predicting and confirming will force the learner to think about what he or she is going to read before actually seeing the print. This strategy also helps the learner to read with purpose—to find out whether his or her predictions were right.

27. Mystery Words

Note: You may want to use this strategy along with Strategy 20, "Riddles."

Description
A nonsense "mystery" word is substituted for the name of a person, place, or thing. The learner must read and work through clues, sentence by sentence, to determine what the mystery word is.

Directions

1. Make up a story about a person, place, or thing. Use the mystery word in your title. For example:

    Goosh
    Goosh is my favorite food.
    There are many types of goosh.
    Goosh comes in various sizes.
    I had goosh at my birthday party.
    Some of my friends burned their
    mouths when they ate the goosh.
    I like a lot of cheese on my goosh.
    My friend likes pepperoni on her goosh. (Pizza)

    Yukky Yukkers
    I am a yukky yukker.
    I live in your home.
    I like it when you leave your house in a mess.
    Please don't do your dishes.
    Please leave your food out.
    I like to eat anything, even garbage.
    I don't like bright lights; I usually come out when it's dark.
    People don't like me.
    They try to kill me with powders and sprays.
    I am black and buggy. (Cockroach)

2. Use a sheet of paper to cover up the story except for the title and first line. Ask the learner to make predictions based on these. Write down the predictions.

3. Uncover the second line and ask the learner to read it. Return to the predictions and cross out any the learner thinks are definitely wrong. Encourage new predictions.

4. Uncover the next line. Again cross out predictions the learner thinks are wrong and encourage new ones.

5. Repeat this procedure throughout the remaining lines until the mystery word is discovered.

6. Ask which words offered the best clues in helping the learner decide what the mystery word stood for.

7. Point out and discuss how certain key words carried most of the meaning.

Instructional Principle
This strategy causes the learner to think before actually seeing the print. It reinforces the fact that one reads much faster and more efficiently *and* gains more meaning if he or she predicts.

28. Sandwich Instructions

Description
The learner reads and follows directions on how to make a sandwich.

Directions

1. Give the learner a set of written instructions on how to make a sandwich. For example:

    A. To make a peanut butter and jelly sandwich, take one slice of bread from a loaf.
    B. Pick up a knife.
    C. Stick the knife into the peanut butter and cover one-half of the slice of bread with peanut butter.
    D. Stick the knife into jelly and cover the other half of the bread with jelly.
    E. Fold the bread in half, with the jelly side on top of the peanut butter side.
    F. Eat the sandwich (if you like peanut butter and jelly sandwiches).

2. Ask the learner to write the directions for a different peanut butter and jelly sandwich. When he or she has done so, read and follow them.

Instructional Principle
To follow directions, the learner must read for meaning. Almost everyone has made a peanut butter and jelly sandwich, so the reading is simplified. However, notice that the example directions are slightly unusual. Your learner will have to think before acting.

29. Drawing an Object

Description
The learner reads simple written directions on how to draw an object and then draws that object.

Directions

1. Give the learner a set of written directions like the following:

    A. Draw an *X* in the middle of the page.
    B. Draw a square around the *X* so that all four corners of the square
       stouch all four ends of the *X*.
    C. Draw a small circle in the right-hand corner of the page.
    D. Write your name on the bottom left side of the paper

2. Ask the learner to write new directions for you to follow.

Instructional Principle
As with Strategy 28, the learner must read carefully and for meaning.

30. Miscue Analysis

Description
Tape the learner while he or she is reading a story and then play the tape
back for both of you to hear. Analyze the mistakes (miscues [deviations
from the author's words]) together. This activity allows the learner to
become aware of his or her error patterns.

Directions

1. Select a passage that is at the learner's instructional level and have
    him or her read the passage into a tape recorder. Allow the learner
    to read without corrections or interruptions from you.

2. Play the tape back and ask the learner to follow along and stop the
    tape every time he or she hears a miscue.

3. If the learner does not hear a miscue, stop the tape yourself and point
    out the problem.

4. Discuss each miscue to determine if it changes the meaning of the
    sentence.

5. If the miscue changes the meaning, discuss how and why the
    meaning was altered.

6. If the miscue does not change the meaning, do not be concerned.
    Compliment the learner for not changing the meaning and continue
    playing the tape.

Instructional Principle
This strategy teaches the learner how both to recognize and to correct

his or her miscues. It helps readers develop an awareness of their reading habits. This awareness is a critical part of improving a learner's reading ability.

31. Brainstorming Before Reading

Description
Select a passage about a subject that is familiar and of interest to the learner. Ask the learner to tell you everything he or she knows about the subject before reading the text and to keep this information in mind as he or she reads.

Directions

1. Locate a passage about a subject that the learner knows and cares about.

2. Ask the learner to tell you everything he or she knows about the subject. Write this information on paper or on the chalkboard.

3. Discuss the importance of keeping this information in mind as the learner reads.

4. Explain that people can read more quickly and effectively when they already know about a subject.

5. Ask the learner to read the article quickly to see if there is any information he or she did not know or if there is any incorrect information.

6. Discuss the content of the article with the learner.

Instructional Principle
The more one knows about a subject, the easier it is to read about. While good readers intuitively activate their knowledge about a topic when they read, poor readers seldom rely on their own knowledge and experience. The brainstorming strategy forces the learner to think first, then read.

CHAPTER

6

Profile Four Readers and Teaching Strategies

PROFILE FOUR LEARNERS might best be characterized as adults and adolescents who need just a little help with reading and a boost in self-confidence. They have the potential to succeed on the GED Test and at most educational endeavors they choose. (Some of these learners not only pass the GED Test but also continue their education at universities, community colleges, and trade schools.) Profile Four learners are readers with independent levels ranging from fifth to mid-sixth grade; their instructional levels are seventh to low eighth grade; their listening-capacity levels range from ninth to beginning college levels.

The reading problems of Profile Four learners center on reading too slowly and having difficulty with content-area texts. They can read newspapers, short stories, and high-interest articles but have difficulty with social studies, science, and literature selections like those on the GED Test. Unlike the other learners we have discussed, Profile Four learners report that they write somewhat frequently. They are able to write postcards, shopping lists, and short notes with relatively few problems, but longer essay-like writing poses more difficulty. When problems are encountered, these learners feel that spelling causes them the most concern.

Only about one-third of the learners in this profile have been in special-education classes. More of this number appear to have been placed in classes for children with behavior disorders than for those with learning disabilities.

One-third of Profile Four learners have auditory discrimination problems; while over half have vision problems.

Usually these individuals are younger than the other students we've discussed. Many have completed ten or eleven years of school. Women in this profile most often had dropped out of school because of pregnancy. Men appeared to have quit school to work, usually in a family-owned business, or to join the military. Almost 40 percent of the adults in this profile are employed full time, and some have their own businesses.

Over half the learners in Profile Four took the initiative to request testing themselves. Many "just never felt things were right" with respect to their reading abilities. One Profile Four learner ran a successful housecleaning business and managed over forty employees, while another owned a seamstress shop. One man was employed as a guard at a local penitentiary, where GED classes were given. He wondered if he was "smart enough" to pass the test if he enrolled in the course.

These learners could be described as *aliterate*; they *can* read but *choose* not to. Many complain that they would like to read but that reading is "too slow;" therefore, they decide to exclude most print from their lives beyond the local newspaper or television guide.

DIAGNOSTIC PROFILE
Name: Sheila   *Age: 29*

Background Information

Sheila grew up in poverty in East St. Louis, Illinois, and St. Louis, Missouri. After completing ninth grade, she quit school and worked at a number of jobs. Although Sheila has attended reading classes in a variety of settings, she seems to function best with a volunteer tutor.

A married woman, Sheila lives with her husband and two children, ages nine and ten. She feels strongly that she must set a good example for her children. She is enthusiastic about working with her tutor.

Sheila has a history of severe headaches and high blood pressure. This condition is currently being treated with medication.

Reading Ability/View of Reading

Sheila's independent level is estimated to be mid-fifth to low sixth grade. Her instructional level is within the sixth- to seventh-grade range. Her listening-capacity level appears to be eleventh to twelfth grade, possibly higher. Her greatest errors appeared when she confronted words in isolation.

When Sheila read aloud, she read very slowly, word for word, and appeared very insecure. She needed a great deal of reassurance to continue. Although she made several miscues, these usually did not change the meaning of the passage.

Sheila's silent reading was also very slow (she twice requested the pronunciation of a word). Nevertheless, her comprehension was adequate despite the slow reading rate. She has little difficulty reading narrative text, but expository text such as science and social studies give her problems.

When questioned about her approach to reading, Sheila said that when she comes to a word she does not know, she usually asks someone for assistance. If that is not possible, she looks up the word in a dictionary. When she was asked, "Would you ever try skipping the word and reading ahead to see if you could figure it out?" Sheila responded, "No, that would be cheating. I might miss something important."

Sheila stated that it is extremely important for her to become a good reader, as all her friends are. She feels her children will do better in school if she sets a positive example.

Vision/Auditory Discrimination

Sheila wears new glasses for nearsightedness. No problems with auditory discrimination are evident.

Summary

Because she can read independently at the mid-fifth grade to low-sixth grade level, Sheila can read and understand most things she encounters daily. Instructional materials for her should begin with pre-GED books and progress to GED texts. Her listening-capacity level indicates she has the potential to improve greatly, certainly enough to obtain her goal of passing the GED. Lack of secondary schooling and interrupted literacy instruction appear to be the cause of her problems. She brings little prior knowledge to content-area materials, especially science and social studies.

Sheila is representative of Profile Four adults and adolescents. These learners are characterized by the following educational traits.

Profile Four learners—

- Have independent and instructional levels ranging from low fifth to low eighth grade

- Have listening-capacity levels generally ninth grade and above
- Generally have completed ten or more years of school but report poor attendance during those years
- Often lack confidence in their intellectual abilities even though they may be confident and capable in other aspects of their lives

Profile Four learners are characterized by the following personal and environmental data:

- Frequently have a home life that is stable and supportive of their educational endeavors
- Often are employed and sometimes self-employed
- Are highly motivated to improve their reading skills and willing to put forth substantial effort to do so

Profile Four learners need instruction in content-area subjects, especially those found on the GED Test. They should be able to progress rather quickly from pre-GED to GED texts and are strong candidates for additional educational opportunities.

TEACHING STRATEGIES FOR PROFILE FOUR READERS

32. Text Mapping

Description
A text map is a unique type of outline a learner makes after reading an article, a story, or a chapter in a textbook. The learner is required to make relationships between key concepts.

Directions

1. Find an interesting article you feel your student would enjoy reading. After you both read the article silently, you should both decide what the main topic of the article is. Ask him or her to write the main topic on a piece of paper.

2. Next have the learner list key concepts or ideas that relate to the main topic. These should be written below the main topic.

3. On a separate sheet of paper have the learner write the main topic in the center of the page and draw a circle around what he or she has written.

4. Ask the learner to pick the first key concept and put that on the paper, circle it and draw a line from the middle circle to the main topic circle. Then have the learner select the second key concept and decide if that concept relates more to the first key concept or to the main topic. If it relates more closely to the main topic, the learner should list it, draw a circle around it and connect it to the main idea. If it relates more closely to the first key concept, the learner should connect it to that concept.

5. Have the learner continue this procedure until all the key concepts have been listed and connected.

6. Now invite the learner to reread the article to decide if any subtopics need to be listed. If this is the case, ask the learner to list them and connect them to the concepts to which they relate. As an example, suppose the learner has read an article about marriage. The key concepts are love, finances, and companionship. Subtopics include the ideas of support and mature and immature love. (See Figure A.) First, the learner writes *marriage* in the center of the page, as shown. Next the learner writes *love* and places it in a circle connected to

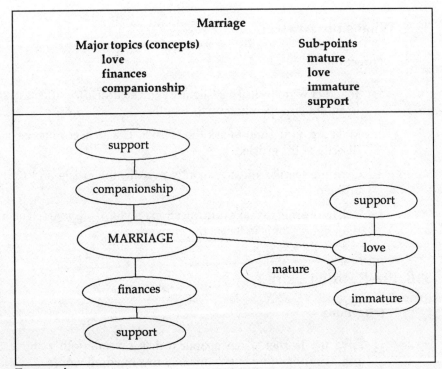

FIGURE A

marriage. *Support* relates to love, finances, and marriage, so the learner lists it and connects it to all three. The learner adds *finances* to the outline, and so on.

7. Ask the learner to explain his or her map to you and revise it if necessary.

Instructional Principle
This strategy requires the learner to read for major concepts and to relate these concepts to one another as well as to the main topic. Information is *related* rather than *separated*, which helps the learner make meaning. In addition, this strategy helps the learner relate specific information to general information.

33. Skimming

Description
Discuss with the learner the importance of being able to identify key words when skimming for information. The following strategies all develop the ability to locate information quickly by skimming.

33A. What's the Answer?

Directions

1. Together with the learner, silently skim an article for fifteen seconds to a minute, depending on its length.

2. Make up a question to ask the learner. The answer must be stated directly in the article.

3. Give the learner fifteen seconds to skim the article and find the answer.

4. Ask the learner to make up a question for you. Give yourself no more than five seconds to locate the answer.

33B. Pre-Reading Skim

Directions

1. Give the learner a newspaper article or some other interesting passage containing approximately five hundred words.

2. Ask the learner to predict what the article will be about based on its title. Write the predictions on an index card.

3. Have the learner skim the passage for five seconds. Then tell him or her to stop and tell you everything he or she remembers about what was read. Write the learner's responses down.

4. Discuss how accurate the learner's predictions were in light of what he or she learned from the five-second skim. Then have the learner make new predictions.

5. Have the learner start at the beginning of the article again and skim it for fifteen seconds. Then ask for anything else he or she learned from this skim. Write the information down. Talk about the accuracy of the predictions this time.

6. Once more, have the learner start at the beginning and skim the article, this time for thirty seconds. Again, write down what the reader has learned and discuss how accurate his or her predictions were.

7. Finally, have the learner read the entire article carefully.

8. Review the list of predictions. With the learner, revise and add to the list, based upon this last careful reading.

9. Point out how accurate a "skim list" can be, even though the learner did not (at first) read carefully.

10. Be patient with this activity. It is sometimes frustrating to readers who have not yet developed the skill of skimming. Try it routinely. After six or eight times, it will be successful.

33C. Headline Match Game

Directions

1. Cut out interesting newspaper or tabloid articles and cut off their headlines.

2. Paste each article onto the bottom half of a sheet of paper and fold the top half over the article. Number each article on the outside of the sheet.

3. Do this with twelve to fifteen articles. If you are using this strategy with a group of learners instead of an individual, have a different article for each member of the group.

4. Scramble the headlines and type them with a letter and blank before each, like this:

      _____ A.   Title of Headline
      _____ B.   Title of Headline

Put them on a ditto master or run some copies of the list so you can use it more than once.

5. Hand the learner the stack of folded, numbered articles.

6. Provide the sheet listing the lettered and scrambled headlines.

7. Give the learner ten seconds to skim the first article. Then ask him or her to stop and mark the blank next to the appropriate headline with the number of the article he or she has just skimmed. Allow five seconds to mark the headline sheet. Then have the learner turn to the next article.

8. Repeat the process, allowing ten seconds for the second article. Again, have the learner mark the blank next to the headline title that matches the article just read.

9. Go through the entire stack of articles in this manner.

10. Compare the learner's responses with the correct ones. Discuss which ones were correct and which were not. Learners enjoy this game and improve after several attempts.

11. If you use this activity with a group, put the group in a circle and give each person one folded, numbered article and a copy of the headline answer sheet. Use the same directions as above, with one exception. When everyone has finished their first article and marked the headline sheet, ask the learners to pass their articles to the left so that all have a new article. Tell them to open it, time them as they skim the article and mark the sheet, then have them pass the article on until all the articles have been read and marked by each learner.

Instructional Principle

Profile Four readers tend to read too slowly; they have trouble with most tests because they cannot access the information in the passages quickly enough. These skimming activities help improve rate and concentration.

34. Key Word Search Strategies

Description

These strategies require the learner to find the key words that carry the meaning of sentences and passages.

34A. Key Word Version

Directions

1. Make up a fairly complex sentence, such as, "A stooped and weary old man in faded blue jeans came to the door looking for work."

2. Ask the learner to read the sentence and briefly tell what it said.

3. Use a pen or magic marker and black out all but the essential words in the sentence (*man, came, looking, work*). While you do this, ask the learner to write a shortened version of the sentence using the key words. Then compare the two versions to see if they have the same meaning. Discuss any differences.

34B. Key Word Search

Directions

1. Ask the learner to locate several short passages that you most likely have not read and bring them to the session. You should do the same thing for the learner.

2. Begin this activity by asking the learner to read quickly and silently one of the short passages he or she brought.

3. After the learner has read the passage, have him or her go back and make small check marks above the key words.

4. Instruct the learner to black out every third word checked and read the remaining words aloud to you.

5. Listen and tell the learner what you think the passage is about from these key words. Discuss any differences.

6. Reverse the procedure. This time you select and narrow down key words from a passage.

7. Continue this procedure until you and the learner have each read and discussed three or four passages.

34C. Deletion of Non-Key Words

Directions

1. Give the learner a reading passage in which all the unessential words

have been deleted by you. Leave short blank spaces to indicate where words were present.

2. Ask the learner to read the prepared selection silently.

3. After the learner has read the entire passage, talk about what was read. Then ask the learner to fill in the deleted words.

4. Compare the learner's version with the original text. Discuss any differences.

Instructional Principle

Profile Four readers tend to process *every* word when they read. Coupled with their limited prior knowledge, this tendency makes them read too slowly to gain meaning. These strategies demonstrate how to locate key words, which will increase reading speed and improve comprehension.

35. Key Word Predicting Strategies

Note: You may want to use these strategies along with Strategy 24, "Phrase Chunking and Key Word Identification," and Strategies 34A–34C, "Key Word Search Strategies."

Description

The following strategies help develop the learner's ability to predict what will happen in a reading selection by making use of key words.

35A. Key Word Comic Strips

Directions

1. Cut comic strips into frames and paste each frame to an index card.

2. Pick out and list one key word from each comic strip frame. Write this key word on the other side of the index card.

3. Show the learner the key word from frame one. Ask him or her to predict what will take place in frame one.

4. Let the learner see frame one for five seconds and then make any changes he or she wishes.

5. Continue this procedure with each frame, allowing only five seconds per frame.

6. Provide the learner with all the comic strip frames. Discuss the accuracy of his or her predictions.

35B. Key Word Story Categorizing

Directions

1. Locate a short story that will interest the learner. Select key words from the story and put them into the following categories: setting, characters, problem, plot, and ending.

2. Show these category key words to the learner and ask him or her to predict what the story will be about. Jot down these predictions.

3. Ask the learner to read the story to confirm the predictions. Discuss the correct predictions; if there were also incorrect predictions, discuss why they were incorrect.

35C. Key Word Predicting

Directions

1. Select an article of five hundred to seven hundred words. (Initially, the articles should be of high interest to the learner; later, you can choose articles that focus more on content such as science or social studies.)

2. Identify twelve to fifteen key words from the article. Be sure these words carry the major points and meaning. Write these words on an index card.

3. Show the card to the learner and ask him or her to make predictions about the article's content.

4. Ask the learner to read the article and determine how close the predictions were.

5. After you've used this strategy several times, reverse the procedure and invite the learner to bring an article with selected key words for you to read.

Instructional Principle
These key-word predicting strategies are designed to help readers think before they see. This forces purposeful reading; making predictions involves readers because they want to read in order to find out whether they were right or wrong. In addition, this activity helps the reader learn what key words are, how they carry meaning, and how to find them. Key-word strategies help readers become more efficient meaning-makers.

36. Summarizing Strategies

Description
These summarizing strategies require readers to reduce all the information read into a statement of the main idea.

36A. About Point

Directions

1.   Select an interesting paragraph and have the learner read it.

2.   Ask the learner to tell what the paragraph is about in one or two words.

3.   Expand the points made by those two words to seven or eight words that tell the main idea of the paragraph. For example:

About: _____   _____
Point: ____ ____ ____ ____
       ____ ____ ____ ____

36B. Gist (Cunningham 1982)

Directions

1.   Select a paragraph that will interest the learner.

2.   Ask the learner to read the first sentence and summarize it in five words or less.

3.   Ask the learner to read the second sentence and then summarize *both* sentences in eight words or less.

4.   Ask the learner to read the third sentence and then summarize all three sentences in fifteen words or less.

5.   Continue for the remainder of the paragraph to produce one sentence of fifteen words or less that best summarizes the paragraph.

Instructional Principle
The ability to summarize the main idea of a paragraph is difficult for poor readers. Yet this skill is an important part of the GED Test and others like it. These strategies, along with the key-word strategies, help readers chunk information in different ways.

37. Retellings

Description
Retellings require the learner to summarize in his or her own words. There are no questions to answer. Cued retellings provide key-word help for the summary, while open retellings provide no such assistance.

Note: See Key Word Strategies 34 and 35 for help with the groundwork for these two strategies.

37A. Cued Retelling

Directions

1. Select an article about two to five pages long and ask the learner to read it.

2. Provide the learner with ten or fifteen key words from the story.

3. Invite the learner to write a retelling of the story using all the key words you selected.

37B. Open Retelling

Directions

1. Select a short story about two to five pages long and ask the learner to read it.

2. After the story is read, ask the learner to select ten to fifteen key words and jot them down.

3. Invite the learner to write a retelling using all of his or her key words. Explain that using key words helps identify the main idea and the main points of an article.

Instructional Principle
Profile Four readers often are good word callers. They correctly read all the words but have no idea of the meaning of what they have read. Retellings require these readers to make meaning on their own. Therefore, it's best to start with cued retellings and then gradually switch to open retellings.

38. Following Directions

Description

The learner is provided with directions on how to play a game. He or she reads the directions and then explains how to play the game.

38A. Game Directions

Directions

1. Pick a game that is fairly easy, but one you think the learner will want to learn to play (Monopoly, Trivial Pursuit, Boggle, and so on).

2. Ask the learner to read the directions and then explain to you or a partner how to play the game.

3. Begin to play the game, doing exactly what the learner instructs you to do. If the game is not working out, ask him or her to reread and retell the directions until the game is played properly.

38B. Missing Directions

Directions

1. Locate a simple set of instructions for a game or a recipe. Write these down but leave out an important part.

2. Ask the learner to read these instructions, allowing him or her to discover that something important is missing.

3. Discuss how the learner knew what was missing. The following is an example of such instructions:*

> We each put our cards in a pile.
> We both turn over the top card in our pile.
> We look at the cards to see who has the special card.
> Then we turn over the next card in our pile to see who has the special card this time.
> In the end, the person with the most special cards wins the game.

These instructions are incomplete because we have failed to identify what the "special card" might be.

---

*From Baker and Brown, 1980.

Instructional Principle
These two strategies require Profile Four learners to make sense of a relatively complicated series of directions. They are motivated to make sense of the directions because there is a payoff—they learn a new game or a new recipe as a result.

39. Insert

Description
As the learner reads, he or she inserts a symbol in the margin to indicate his or her reaction to the article.

Directions

1. Select an article regarding a topic about which the learner will have strong opinions or interest.

2. Ask the learner to read the article and insert in the margin either a star or a question mark (* or ?). A star in the margin means the learner is reading something he or she feels is particularly important. A question mark in the margin indicates something he or she feels is confusing or hard to follow.

3. Once the learner is through reading and marking, discuss what he or she felt was important and what was confusing.

4. Help the learner understand the confusing sections.

5. Variations of this activity might use the following symbols (or you can make up your own):

   !! = strongly agree
   XX = strongly disagree
   ∪ = that's funny
   ∩ = that's sad
   → = this is important

Instructional Principle
Poor readers often establish no purpose in their reading; they just read words. Good readers read with a purpose. This simple marking system creates a specific purpose in the reader. It forces the learner to interact with the text in a meaningful way.

40. SQ3R

Description
This strategy is a procedure for studying content-area text. It includes five steps: survey, question, read, recite, and review. SQ3R is a time-honored technique that has been used for the last forty years (Robinson 1946).

Directions

1. Select a passage from a content-area text at an appropriate reading level.

2. Explain to the learner the five steps in the strategy.

    A. *S = Survey*. Explain how to skim the entire passage to get an overall feel for its content. Headings, pictures, and other graphics should be studied.

    B. *Q = Question*. Once the passage has been skimmed, direct the learner to go to the first major heading and turn it into questions. The questions are easier to form if they start with the five *w*'s (*who, what, where, when, why*). For example, a heading may be "The Process of Photosynthesis." Appropriate questions might be: What is photosynthesis? Where does photosynthesis take place? When does photosynthesis happen? Why does photosynthesis occur?

    C. *R = Read*. The learner reads the passage under the heading to answer his or her own questions.

    D. *R = Recite*. Ask the learner to answer the questions orally or in writing. Encourage the learner to answer in his or her own words rather than copy from the text.

    E. *R = Review*. The learner reviews the questions formed from each section heading and attempts to recall the information and put it together into a coherent whole.

Instructional Principle
SQ3R creates a purpose for reading by requiring the learner to create his or her own questions and then read to find answers to these questions. Good readers automatically read purposefully to answer their own questions. Profile Four learners are often motivated to read content-area material using this strategy.

CHAPTER
7

Questions We Are Frequently Asked

WE HOPE OUR BOOK has helped you find answers to many of the problems and concerns you have about teaching reading. If questions remain, perhaps you'll find them answered in this chapter.

Q: Most of your strategies do not include much oral reading. How much oral reading should I be doing with my learner?

A: Oral reading is not an important part of the strategies because it differs greatly from silent reading. When you read orally, you focus on the *act* of reading out loud: Oral reading makes reading a *performance*. In addition, oral reading is much slower than silent reading. Under these conditions, you cannot totally concentrate on the purpose of reading—comprehension.

Oral reading should be used cautiously and generally only under the following conditions: when reading poetry, plays, radio scripts, or other material meant to be read aloud with expression; when practicing a speech that will actually be read orally; or when reading for assessment purposes.

Q: Most of your strategies are designed to be used in a one-on-one situation. I have twenty learners. How can I modify your suggestions to fit my situation?

A: Almost all the strategies can be used with larger groups. Instead of putting responses on paper or cards, you can use a blackboard or an overhead projector with a group. With guidance, learners can often do the activities and strategies themselves. Invite your learners to pair off or to form small groups.

Q: I teach junior high school. Will your suggestions help younger learners?

A: All the strategies suggested in this book have been used successfully with elementary, secondary, and adult students. You can modify the subject matter to suit the interests and needs of your students.

Q: You seldom recommend specific instructional materials. How do I choose these?

A: Two types of materials are recommended. First, real-world materials are abundant. Tabloids such as the *National Enquirer* and the *Globe* obtained at your supermarket checkout are popular with learners, though you'll want to select articles prudently. *USA Today* and local newspapers are also favorites. Magazines such as *Reader's Digest, Car and Driver,* and *Jet* work well too. The important thing to remember is to use *real* catalogs, *real* menus, *real* job application forms, and other *real* materials your learner wishes to read.

Second, a wealth of commercial materials contain interesting stories that many learners enjoy. Don't shy away from commercial materials simply because you do not like the lesson plans provided. You can use the strategies in this book with commercial materials instead of the exercises provided by the publisher.

Q: The learner I tutor does not fit exactly into any of your profiles. Should I use strategies from more than one profile?

A: Of course. The profiles tend to fit the majority of the learners we have observed, but we do not intend to label all readers. Pick those strategies from any of the profiles that will best meet the needs of your learner.

Q: How long should tutoring sessions be, and how often should they be held?

A: Daily sessions of 1 hour to 1½ hours are the ideal, but that is seldom realistic. If possible, two 1½-hour sessions per week are desirable. Planning takes a great deal of time, however, and most instructors have busy schedules. Your tutoring schedule depends upon your individual situation. The important thing to remember is that your learner must practice reading a *minimum* of 7 hours per week if progress is to be made. Therefore, you must plan materials for your learner to read when you are not present. Don't overlook the value of recording stories on tape, so that your learner can practice them independently.

Q: Your strategies and approach are much different from the techniques I have been using. How do I know they will work?

A: We can understand this concern. Fortunately, we have received positive comments and evaluations from over two hundred ABE instructors and volunteer tutors. Our research indicates that adults who were able to change their view of reading from a phonetic or a word-bound approach to one of searching for meaning improved three to four times faster than learners who were not instructed with meaning-making strategies (Keefe and Meyer 1980; Meyer and Keefe 1985; Meyer, Keefe, and Bauer 1986). These gains take time to accomplish. That is why we stress the Good Reader Strategies and the importance of sharing the theory of each strategy with learners.

Appendix

Performance Levels of Profiles*

	Profile One	Profile Two	Profile Three	Profile Four
Estimated independent reading levels	Nonreader	Pre-first	Low-second to low-third grade	Low-fifth to mid-sixth grade
Estimated instructional reading levels	Pre-first to low-first grade	Pre-first to mid-first grade	Low-third to low-fourth grade	Upper-sixth to low-eighth grade
Estimated listening-capacity levels	Pre-first to low-second grade	Mid-fifth to mid-seventh grade	Low-sixth to mid-seventh grade	Ninth grade and above

Characteristics of Profiles (as percentage in profile)**

	Profile One	Profile Two	Profile Three	Profile Four
As sounds (phonics)	49%***	55%***	48%	50%
As words	15	28	32	23
As meaning	3	3	30	25
Frequency of vision problems	85	68	60	52
Frequency of auditory discrimination problems	70	40	36	32

*This data is based upon the diagnostic testing of 247 adults.

**Specific percentages may change as the authors' data base grows, but we do not feel general trends will change.

***Some members in Profile One and Profile Two were unable to respond.

Suggested Readings

The following books are ones we have found especially helpful.

Literacy Issues

Harman, David. *Illiteracy: A National Dilemma*. Cambridge, 1987.

Hunter, Carman St. John, and Harman, David. *Adult Illiteracy in the United States*. McGraw-Hill, 1978.

Kozol, Jonathan. *Illiterate America*. Doubleday, 1985.

Ungerleider, Dorothy. *Reading, Writing, and Rage*. Jalmar Press, 1985.

Teaching Reading

Goodman, Kenneth. *What's Whole in Whole Language?* Heinemann, 1986.

Goodman, Kenneth; Smith, E. Brooks; Meredith, Robert; and Goodman, Yetta. *Language and Thinking in School: A Whole Language Curriculum*. 3rd ed. Richard C. Owen, 1987.

Smith, Frank. *Reading Without Nonsense*. 2nd ed. Teacher's College Press, 1985.

Weaver, Constance. *Reading Process and Practice: From Socio-Psycholinguistics to Whole Language*. Heinemann, 1988.

References

Baker, Linda, and Brown, Ann L. *Metacognitive Skills and Reading*. Technical Report No. 188. Center for the Study of Reading, 1980.

Burke, Carolyn. Written conversation in *The Authoring Cycle: A Viewing Guide*. Edited by Jerome Harste, Kathryn Mitchell Pierce, and Trevor Cairney. Heinemann, 1985.

Cooper, Charles R., and Petrosky, Anthony R. "A Psycholinguistic View of the Fluent Reading Process." *Journal of Reading* 20 (1976): 184–207.

Cunningham, James W. "Generating Interactions Between Schemata and Text." In *New Inquiries in Reading Research and Instruction*. Thirty-first Yearbook of the National Reading Conference, edited by J. A. Niles and Louis Harris. National Reading Conference, 1982, 42–47.

Ginsburg, Herbert, and Opper, Sylvia. *Piaget's Theory of Intellectual Development: An Introduction*. Prentice-Hall, 1969.

Goodman, Kenneth; Smith, E. Brooks; Meredith, Robert; and Goodman, Yetta. *Language and Thinking in School: A Whole Language Curriculum*. 3rd ed. Richard C. Owen, 1987.

Johns, Jerry. *Basic Reading Inventory*, 3rd ed. Kendall-Hunt, 1985.

Jordan, Dale R. *Dyslexia in the Classroom*, 2nd ed. Charles E. Merrill Publishing Co., 1977.

Jordan, William C. "Prime-O-Tec: The New Reading Method." *Academic Therapy Quarterly* 2 (no. 4) (1967): 248–50.

Keefe, Donald, and Meyer, Valerie. "Adult Disabled Readers: Their Perceived Models of the Reading Process." *Adult Literacy and Basic Education* 4 (1980): 120–24.

Meyer, Valerie, and Keefe, Donald. "Models of the Reading Process Held by ABE and GED Instructors." *Reading Horizons* 25 (1985): 133–36.

Meyer, Valerie; Keefe, Donald; and Bauer, Gail. "Some Basic Principles of the Reading Process Required of Literacy Volunteers." *Journal of Reading* 29 (1986): 544–48.

Robinson, F. P. *Effective Study*. Harper and Brothers, 1946.

Slosson, Richard L. *Slosson Intelligence Test*. Slosson Educational Publications, Inc. 1984.

Smith, Frank. *Reading Without Nonsense*. 2nd ed. Teacher's College Press, 1985.

Weaver, Constance. *Reading Process and Practice: From Socio-Psycholinguistics to Whole Language*. Heinemann, 1988.

Wepman, Joseph M. *Auditory Discrimination Test*. 2nd ed. Western Psychological Services, 1986.

Index